The People's History

# Widdrington and Stobswood

by

Neil Taylor

## Dedication

This book is dedicated to our dear Erin 1986-2004,
A lovely young lady, this is the poem she wrote.

I am a dreamer and I dream
I don't intend to stop anytime soon
Because without dreams
The real world would be far too real.

*Erin Foster*

# Contents

Outside the old Widdrington Hotel, the ladies of the Women's Institute sit on a bed of hay aboard a farm cart pulled by a local farmer's Clydesdale horse. Their destination Druridge Bay on an annual outing in 1928. The ladies known are, from left: Mary Laidlaw, Dot Laidlaw and Eleanor Laidlaw.

## Acknowledgements

**Contributors**

Louise Curry (Widdrington Regeneration Initiative), Captain Francis N. Widdrington, George Lamb (North East Co-op Archives), Widdrington Park Group, George Nairn, Bill Kell, Jim Bolton Snr, Jim Bolton Jnr, Alec Gordon, Rudi Lux, Tommy Brown, Margaret Brown, John Redpath, Nancy Stewart, John Talbot, Mike Kirkup, George Mavin, Bob Mavin, Annie McIinness, Betty Britton, Isobel Wyness, Derek Foggo, Gwen Keen, Lindy King, Ernie Moore, John Elliott, Gordon Willoughby, Peter Millar, Cliff Stanbury, Jim Calder, Lil Nicholson, Steve Redpath, David Gagie, Bob Waddell, Ken Walton, Hughie Weallans, Margaret Noble, Keith Noble, Peggy Portsmouth, Kath Hyslop, Stan Lodge, Pat Lodge, Don Short, Barry Waller, Brian Riddell, Raymond Brotherton, Jennifer Clark, Jim Black, Peter Carmichael, Joy Wood, Edith Morgan, Jean Davidson, Audrey King, Irene Sage, Flora Smith, Alice Richardson, Arnott Hope, Annie Hope, Norma Rutter, Finbar O'Driscoll, Stewart Hogg, John Tweddle, Enid and Eddie Dunn, Irene Robertson, Pat Gibbon, Tom McKenna, Harry and Linda Charlton, Margaret Spratt, Mary Willis, Jenny Rochester, Joyce Smith, Mr & Mrs Brotherton, Bridget Gubbins and Andrew Gooding.

Special thanks to Andrew Clark, Jim Stephenson, and my son Neil for their expertise in assisting with the publication of this book.


**Sources**

Ashington Coal Company Records
Beamish Museum
Woodhorn Museum
Morpeth Herald. Morpeth Library
Grangewood First School
Newcastle Central Library
Stobswood &Widdrington Parish Council
Morpeth & Melton Park County Records

*North Miners History*, J. Davison
*Great North Coalfield*, Atkinson
*Rise of British Coal Industry*, J. Nev
*History Coal Mining Britain*, Galloway
*Hodgson's History Northumberland*

*Page One*: John Hogg of Ferneybeds lived in Sanderson and Liddell Terrace during the 1920s and like lots of colliers kept a garden for veg and flowers along with his beehives marked with his initials and home village. John is seen inspecting his hives with son John on his left.



First published in 2004

ISBN 1 902527 37 2

# Introduction

This book is about the villages and enclaves of the Widdrington and Stobswood area, some of which have simply vanished into the mists of time. When I was asked in 2003 by ex Widdrington residents to consider recording the area's history with a view to producing a book, I did so with some trepidation which has long since disappeared as the book progressed and I met up with some wonderful folk and made many new friends along the way. There is a warmth and humour about the people of local mining communities that I have yet to find anywhere else and this comes across in many of their stories.

That a book on this area was long overdue, there is no doubt about that and hopefully this publication will have gone a little way to laying that ghost. After my own research, always a necessary part of the process, I have met and encouraged as many as possible local and former residents both old and new to become involved in the publication, and used their memories, thoughts, photos and memorabilia, this way the final outcome becomes a real History of and for the People.

Many old and in some cases unique photos appear in all the sections and there are also ones more recent and events that deserve to be included because of the intense interest they generated and let's not forget, yesterday is today's history. All of the settlements recorded here have a connection with each other, be it Church, Chapel, Schooling Agriculture, Mining, Recreation or Sport there is a bonding that still exists today and none more strongly than in the people of the lost Colliery villages of Widdrington and Stobswood.

Hopefully there is at least one section in this book that will appeal and folk can associate with and I have done as much as I can to encourage local communities to participate in some way. From the ancient Village of the Widdringtons to the sleepy coastal hamlet of Low Chibburn and Druridge, on to the 19th century pit communities of Widdrington and Stobswood. The Station with its rail link and 20th century housing and the little enclave of Ferneybeds with its Colliery long since gone but still retaining its four rows of houses by the mile long road. Opencast Coal Mining has touched the lives of all of the villages and its people in so many different ways for over 60 years.

There is much more to come from this area, I have only scratched the surface, but hope that this will generate further interest and discussion in the villages. There are some of the contributors to this publication who have sadly not survived to see the end result but will not be forgotten for the assistance they gave me, to these good folk my eternal gratitude.

As far as I am aware all of the photos and memorabilia in this edition are free of copyright restriction, if there is an infringement it is not intended and I can only apologise.

*Neil Taylor*

# Widdrington Chapelry's Early History

The village is an Anglo Saxon settlement, the name from 'Wudheres' People' later Wodrington then Wotheryngton or Wytherington. Other sources revealed in my research suggest the name derives from Wode Ring Tonn and means a Village In The Wood, part of the great forest that existed in ancient times and stretched from Chevington to Earsdon in the South. Once part of the Warkworth Chapelry in medieval days, the 19th century Widdrington Chapelry included Druridge and Linton in the Parish of Woodhorn and was bounded by Ellington and Cresswell to the East, Old Moor to the South and Ulgham to the West. The first evidence of the Widdrington family recorded here was in the 1150s. However there is a possibility that they were a family of the original Angles who came from the Danish/German borders and settled well before the Norman Conquest and were allowed to retain their estate. The forenames of the early Widdringtons bears out this theory, they were certainly not Norman in origin.

Whatever their lineage, what is known is that the family were staunch Catholics and married into other Northumbrian Catholic families obtaining wealth and power. Their Widdrington estate in the Middle Ages comprised of 6,000 acres of mainly parkland with a fine deer herd.

The Widdringtons lost their estates after William, the fourth Lord, was captured at Preston fighting against the Roundheads in 1716. His life was spared but the crown sold the land to the York Building Co in 1720, after some 600 years of Widdrington occupation.

The estate was then acquired by the Warren-Vernons and Sir George Warren had the trees removed and the land tilled. Although small plots had been mined for coal in the 1600s it was now that a Castle Colliery was established in the 1720s. A census for 1801 shows a population of 446 persons.

In 1821 the whole estate now consisted of 4,142 acres in the Chapelry described as a fine corn growing area with a mill at Linton and abundant coal reserves in the domain. The whole Chapelry contained only 388 people and 74 families. and in 1851 this had risen to an estimated 429 people

When Lord Vernon inherited the land in 1855 the Annett family were farming, Mathew Bell was postmaster, Margaret Foster was licensee of the Vernon Arms, John Muers was keeper of the castle, Robert Potts a shoemaker and Henry Strong recorded as a coal agent.

In 1866 a map of the area shows that the village had several small houses, a Home Farm, Trinity Church, Presbyterian Chapel, the Vernon Arms, a Post Office and a Smithy plus the Castle Colliery. Four Farms are shown including Houndalee and the Station and house at Widdrington Station. In 1871 the estate was purchased by Hugh Taylor of Chipchase Castle. Widdrington Colliery commenced operations in 1868, Stobswood Colliery in 1875 and Ferneybeds in 1909. Opencast coal production began at Ferneybeds in 1943 and has continued in the immediate vicinity of the villages up to the present day.

There is no doubt that Widdrington Station, Stobswood, Ferneybeds and Widdrington Colliery grew with the arrival of the railways to the area in 1847 and the sinking of the Chapelry's pits that would see almost a century of deep mine coal production in the area. The Station became an important link with convenient transport for farming stock, coal export and the people themselves to Morpeth, Blyth, Newcastle and Amble.

**SECTION ONE**

# OLD WIDDRINGTON VILLAGE AND DRURIDGE

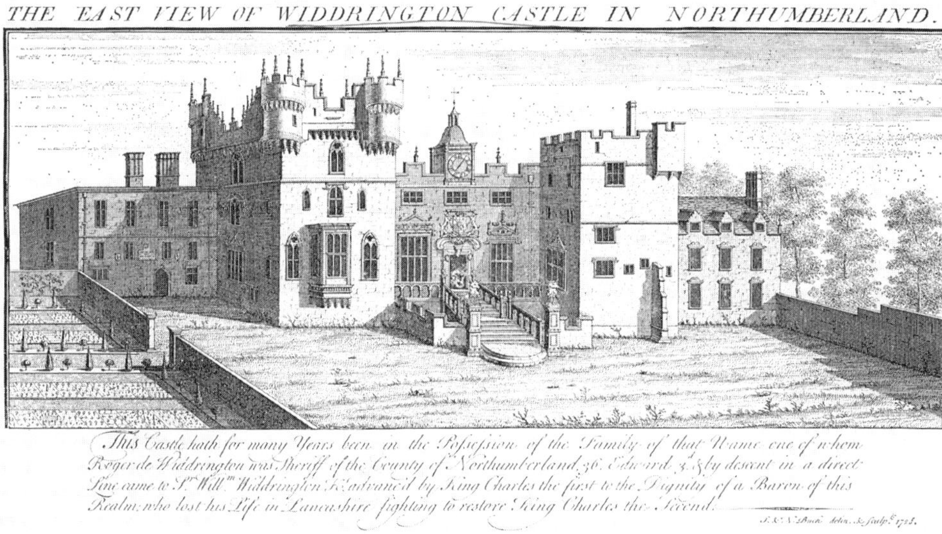


The first Widdrington Castle as engraved by S&N Buck in 1728. Built in a similar style to Chipchase and old Belsay Castle note the overhanging crennelated bartizans and the family Widdrington crest, a bull's head on the entrance pillars. The family coat of arms is above the main east entrance doorway. An avenue of Lime trees named the 'Twelve Apostles' leading to the Castle can be seen to the rear.

Some eight miles north east of Morpeth lies the sylvan little village of Widdrington. Built around a sandstone knoll, it has fine views of Cheviot to the North, Simonside to the West and the long bay of Druridge to the East. Any casual visitor to the village noting the battle scars of opencast working and plant that envelope the area it may seem highly unlikely that a castle was ever sited here or a noble family second only to the proud Percys made this their ancestral home. They would have been mistaken as Widdrington boasted not only one castle but three during a period of 500 years and occupied by the Widdrington family for almost 400 of these. The first and the grandest of the castles crennelated in 1341 would have been preceded by a mansion or tower house dating back to at least the 12th century.

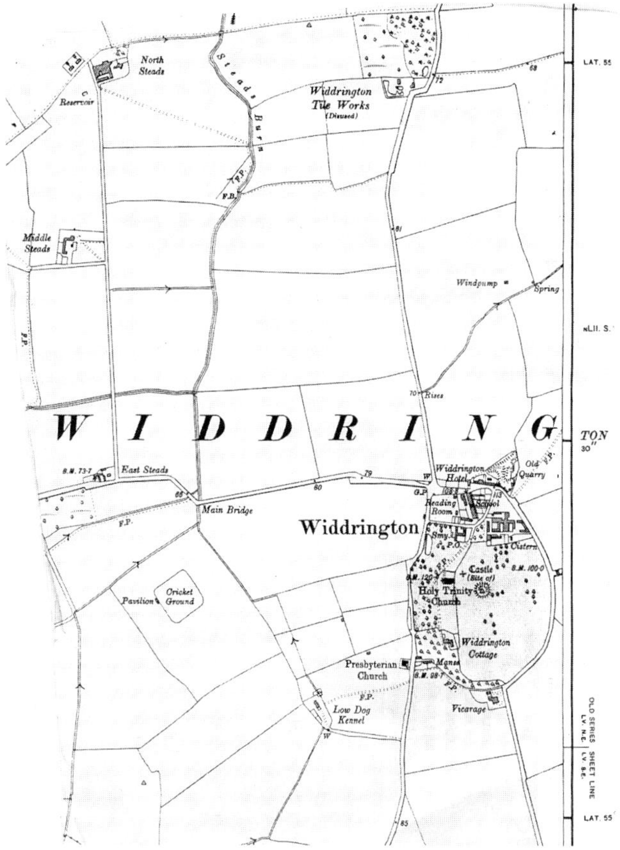


The village as it was in 1925 still a quiet rural retreat.

The crest, a black bull's head also used by other prominent Northumbrian families.

The Widdrington family Coat of Arms Quarterly Argent (Silver) and Jules (Red) with a Sable (Black) bend over all.

In 1691 a surprise attack on the castle which had survived centuries of border warfare was carried out by a French raiding party led by Claude de Forbin under the command of the infamous Jean Bart who had sailed up the East Coast and anchored his ship in Druridge Bay. Unfortunately the Widdringtons were not at home and the French looted the castle and fired stables and barns. On returning to their ship they razed Low Chibburn Perceptory and Widdrington's Dower House lying one mile to the North East.

After William Widdrington was captured fighting the Roundheads at Preston in 1716 his estates were confiscated and sold to the York Building Co in 1720 and later to the Warren Vernon family. The old castle fell into disrepair and was pulled down by Sir George Warren around 1770. He proceeded to build a replica on the old site which was almost complete when it was gutted by fire in 1772. Once again work started on building a new castle but this the third of the Widdrington Mansion Houses erected on a mound close by was not on the same grand scale as the original. Historian John Hodgson described it as 'a slight fantastical insulated building possessing neither grandeur nor convenience', a further report described it as an 'apology for a castle'. This building was demolished in 1862 and the stone used by Lord Vernon to rebuild Widdrington Village and most of the farms.

The second castle was built in 1772 by Sir George Warren on similar lines to the first and destroyed by fire. Note the position of the first two castles which were built much nearer to the Church than the last which occupied a mound to the east.

The last of the castles at Widdrington from an engraving from Hodgson's *History of Northumberland* 1820. The mound can still be seen to the east of the Holy Trinity Church.

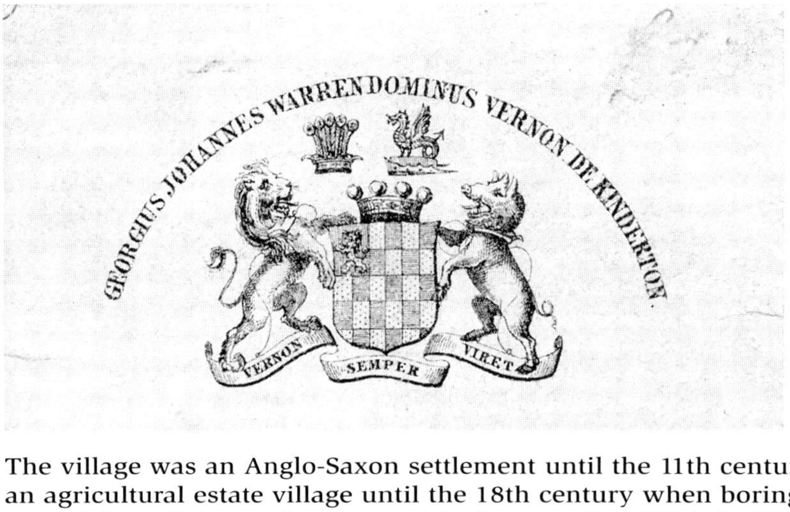


*Left*: The Warren and Vernon coat of Arms. The family also held land in Newbiggin and the counties of Cheshire, Derbyshire and Staffordshire.

The village was an Anglo-Saxon settlement until the 11th century then purely an agricultural estate village until the 18th century when boring operations proved the existence of coal seams in the area. In 1722 John Wake under the direction of Richard Peck bored for coal and found two seams of six inches thick and one of 18 inches before striking a seam of three foot thick at a depth of 156 feet. A major rebuild of the cottages was carried out by Landlord the fifth Lord Vernon in 1862. Living in the village at that time were John Taylor, Grocer and Postmaster. Robert Forster, Butcher. Thomas Robson, Tailor. Ellen Humble, Dressmaker. John Kinghorn, Rabbit Catcher. Francis Urpeth, Joiner. George Watson, Blacksmith. George Lang, Widdrington Hotel. The Widdrington

Association consisted of Lord Vernon, Mr Annett, Mr Mather of Hemscott, Mr Linn of Linton, Mr Urpeth, and Mr Aynsley of Ferneybeds. A branch of the Widdrington and Acklington Co-op Society was opened here in the 1920s. Below is a copy of the sale catalogue of 1871 when Lord Vernon sold the estate to Hugh Taylor of Chipchase.

Farmers in 1887 were recorded as Annetts H. & L. of Chibburn, Annett H. Jacob Widdrington Farm, Annett John W. Houndalee and West Chevington. The soil was described as rich strong and clayey suitable for pasture and tillage. Doctor Frank Gunn was the area doctor, surgeon and medical officer in 1897, with Harry O. Annett listed as an auctioneer living at Houndalee.

In 1938 John Joseph Clark was living at the Manse and Fred White at the Cottage. The rise and fall of deep mine coal extraction and attendant villages in the township can clearly be seen in the census. In 1801 446 folk were recorded, then in 1881 1,038 , and in 1901 it had fallen again to 199 persons.

Preliminary Advertisement.—Northumberland.

HISTORIC TERRITORIAL ESTATE upon the Northumberland Coast, contiguous to the North-Eastern Railway, for sale in the month of July next, in London, by Mr SAMUEL DONKIN,

THE WIDDRINGTON ESTATE,

Having immediate access to the Widdrington Station upon the North-Eastern Railway, and containing nearly

4,000 ACRES

Of rich ox pastures, productive wheat, bean, clover, and turnip lands in several farms, with farm-houses, gardens, policies, and offices, all recently built and designed to meet the requirements of a tenantry in the van of agricultural progress ; intersected by excellent public and private roads, with cottages modelled for the comfort and elevation of the character of the farm labourer. Detached villas of ornate architecture ; thriving plantations.

The entire

VILLAGE OF WIDDRINGTON,

In polished stone and imposing facades, with artizan's and provision shops, reflective ot the consumptive means of an industrious population. The " Vernon Arms," a hostleagium reconciled to the provisions of the " Permissive Bill," under the shadows of a church that has reverberated the anthems of five centuries.

DRURIDGE BAY,

With its broad, open, sandy beach, washing the margin of the estate, and yielding abundantly to the husbandman the fertilising " sea ware."

WIDDRINGTON COLLIERY,

Coining the " black diamonds" with unremitting activity and immediate delivery on to the rail near Chevington Station.

NEWBIGGIN-BY-THE-SEA.

Eight Dwelling Houses, with ground rent of chapel, in the fashionable watering place of Newbiggin.

Also, simultaneously the

STOBSWOOD ESTATE,

A separate property adjoining the Widdrington Estate, with farms, farm houses and offices, containing about 615 acres of arable and pasture lands, and believed to be resting upon a valuable coal seam.

More ample descriptive particulars in future.

Bywell, Felton, April 8, 1871.

Copy of sale of Widdrington Estate.

Widdrington Village

The village in 1903 showing the estate cottages after the major rebuild and the old road system at that period. The small building in the centre was originally a reading room and later a snooker table was added. In later years a man called Lilley ran a garage, seen at the bottom right of the picture.

Annetts Farm as it is today at the heart of the village. The family can be traced back centuries to the tenancy of many of the outlying homesteads.

This impressive little Church whose first phase dates back to the 12th century sits snugly atop a rise. Described simply as a Chapel it would have nestled in the shadows of Widdrington's castles for 700 years.

The Great War Memorial at the Church entrance bears the names of 32 of the Widdrington & District men who gave their lives for their country. Many can be traced to the memorial cemeteries in Flanders.

After the Widdrington family lost their estate in 1716 the Church fell into disrepair and a visit by Archdeacon Sharpe in 1723 found the Church in a deplorable condition as did his son in 1764. Dependent then on the mother Church of Woodhorn, the Archdeacon proposed to Sir George Warren that if he would re-build the Chapel then an endeavour to raise an endowment to retain a resident minister would be sought. John Hodgson in 1826 recorded that there was neither glebe nor parsonage and one Chapel Warden. In the Chapel vault were the dust of three bodies, a man, woman and a child in decaying coffins said to be Lord and Lady Widdrington. Curates can be traced from 1557 when John Scott was registered and also Ralph Errington, Curate of Ulgham in 1828.

**Betty Britton's (née Dodds) Memories**

My dad John Dodds like his father before him was sexton of the Church in the first part of the 1900s. My mam Elizabeth cleaned the Church and twice a year it had to be scrubbed out by hand. All the family walked from our cottage past the Colliery to Church. Farmers would park their horses and gigs outside and in those days all women wore hats in Church and men went bareheaded. It has been known for a woman who forgot her hat to wear a man's cap back to front!

The vicarage was built in 1862 by Lord Vernon at the time that the last of Widdrington's Castles was demolished. An impressive building with landscaped gardens in a decidedly wooded area. Extended in 1876 by new landlord Hugh Taylor the vicariate in 1897 was the Rev William Sykes. Like many other buildings of historical interest the vicarage was pulled down in the mid 20th century.

# Presbyterians

Built in 1765 to cater for the needs of a thriving Puritan community the old Church, on the left of the picture, could accommodate 250 souls. Alterations to the interior in 1829 provided room for 400 congregation.

One of Widdrington's most famous sons John Horsley MA and Presbyterian Minister lived for a time in the village and was a forerunner of the faith in the area until his death in 1732. Theologian, Scientist and Archaeologist his major work was *Britannia Romana* completed shortly before his death. Meetings prior to 1765 were held in members' homes. Records show that the faith progressed apace and a contingent including one of the Annett family set out for London on horseback armed with pistols seeking permission to build a Presbyterian Church in Widdrington.

In 1761 the Rev Alexander Stevenson became the first Minister of the new Church which was completed four years later.

The need for a new Church was evident in the latter part of the 19th century owing to the dilapidated state of the old building. Functions were organised towards the estimated cost of £1100. Land was leased by Lord of the Manor Hugh Taylor and a sum of £100 for a site at the West side of the main road. A foundation stone was laid in September 1893 and the topping out stone settled by the Rev W.L Ross in November with a second stone which was the drawhead from the old Church laid by Mr W. Davison of Coldriffe. The old manse is still used today as a centre for carpet bowls, Girl Guides and a Friendship Club.

The second neat little Presbyterian Church in Gothic style built by Carse and Sons of Amble, is now a United Reformed Church.

*Below*: One of the many events held by Church members to pay off the debt incurred when the Church was built was this Grand Bazzar in 1906 and take a look at the admission charge almost a century ago.

# A GRAND BAZAAR

WILL BE HELD IN

MARQUEES in a FIELD near the PRESBYTERIAN CHURCH,

On JULY 13th and 14th, 1906.

The Stalls will be arranged to represent different Flowers.
Sports and the old time custom of the MAYPOLE, along with INSTRUMENTAL and VOCAL MUSIC will be included in the Programme.

To be Opened on FRIDAY at 3·30 p.m., by

## ALDERMAN W. SUTTON.

Chairman - - Rev. JOHN CRAWFORD, Bedlington.

And on SATURDAY at 2·30 p.m., by

## DR. GUNN.

Prayer by REV. R. R. RIDER.

Chairman - - JOHN JOHNSTON, Esq., Widdrington.

*Admission to Field and Tent on Friday,* **6d.** *Do., Saturday,* **3d.**

(3)

A bevy of Widdrington girls in the late 1930s posing outside the Minister's House. In the row on the left are: Gladys Gibbison, Margaret Walker, Pat Farrell, Winnie Bamburgh. In the row on the right are: Noreen Foggo, Betty Snelgrove, ? Isobel Reed, Evylyn Willis.

Many more young Widdrington children in this snap taken in the Manse grounds also in the 1930s. Included in the back row are: Betty Tate, Betty Snelgrove, Noreen Foggo, Enid Simpson. Middle row: Maureen Snelgrove, Audrey Davison, Jeanette Henry. Second front row: Iris Clarke, Jenny Davison, George Gordon. Front: Billy Tate.

# John Wesley in Widdrington

*Right*: John Wesley champion of the Methodist movement in typical early 18th century preacher's attire.

Widdrington was a favourite place to preach the Gospel for evangelist John Wesley who visited many times during his journeys around the Country in the 18th Century. He was well received by the local farming community who flocked for miles around to hear his service. His account of the afternoon of Monday July 18th 1748 reads. 'We rode to Widdrington it was a delightful evening under the shade of tall trees and every man hung upon the word, none stirred his head or hand, or looked to left or right while I declared in strong terms the grace of our Lord Jesus Christ.' Later he wrote of the earnest congregation here and always a blessing among the people. Methodists world wide celebrated the 300th anniversary of his birth in June 2003.

The Southern approach road to Widdrington in 1911 with the Presbyterian Church on the left and the manse on the right with a horse and trap a popular way to travel then without fear of motor traffic. The Church and manse were not built when Wesley visited nor were there any telegraph poles.

## Village Inn, Arms and Bull

In the early part of the 19th century the old Widdrington Pub was known as the Black Bull the same name as the crest of the Widdrington family, described as an Ale House with Christopher Forster as publican in 1822. Then it was christened the Vernon Arms after the Lord of the Manor. George Lang was mine host in 1862 and Jane Lang held the tenancy in 1938, when it was known as the Widdrington Arms Hotel.

The old Widdrington Arms. Opposite Annetts farm, formerly the Vernon Arms and Black Bull, it was used as a house after closure then demolished when the new Inn was built. Note the estate cottages adjacent in this fine old photo of 100 years ago. Stables were attached to the hostelry and behind a quarry which was filled in by opencast coal works.

The new Widdrington Inn, built by Bill Sanderson of Morpeth in 1939, sits on a prime trading site by the side of the County coastal route, keeps a good pint and serves up some of the best scran in the area. During the Second World War it was used to house Army Officers on exercise in the area.

## Sermons, Songs and Sixpence

Widdrington Village School was Church of England Aided and regular visits by the landowner and vicar were a regular feature on the school curriculum. A record in 1820 shows that Lady Bulkley gave £15 annually to the school and in 1862 Lord Vernon rebuilt the school to cater for 90 children with residence for a master when major alterations took place in the village.

Headmaster in 1887 was Andrew Martin aided by Mrs Martin. The vicar visited on Tuesdays and Wednesdays and recorded that on July 8th 1895 that 'all children were backward, the infants can't write and scarcely know their letters.' When Hugh Taylor and his good lady called on August 23rd, 32 children sang and each child was given sixpence by Mrs Taylor. Religious instruction exams were conducted by the Diocesan Inspector Mr S. Jefferson.

Mary Clapham was head of the school in 1903 when there were 80 children 10 of whom were infants. It was then that the school was closed for six weeks due to a fever epidemic. In 1904 the head was Harry Craig assisted by Jane Costhwaite. The following year the school changed to Public Elementary Status. In 1910 records show Miss C. Robinson as Mistress. The school was used at times during the 1914-18 war and the second world war to accommodate soldiers of various regiments.

In 1939 the old school was in a state of neglect and on the 11th November 1940 schools inspector Mr Firth called to announce the closure of the school. The children would be moved to the Colliery Council School, Stobswood, and Red Row. All desks, piano and sundries removed to Widdrington Council School and on the 20th December 1940 Head Mistress Eleanor G. Davis resigned her charge. A sad day indeed for the village, ironic is it not that we have the same situation in villages throughout the County at the present time.

Well known and respected ladies, Eleanor and Dot Laidlaw, who taught at the village and colliery schools during the 1930s and '40s.

Pat Farrell: 'I lived next door to the school which was only one room and was screened off. We young 'uns got Horlicks every morning, not like the stuff you get today but it came in tablet form and tasted okay. The teachers were Elsie and Dorothy Laidlaw when the school closed and the army took it over in 1940. I had to finish my lessons at the Colliery School.'

Lil Nicholson: 'When I came to the village in 1923 the row never used to be called School Row it was the main part of the village and everyone knew it by that. The schoolhouse was at the end of the row. Mrs Lilley ran a sweetshop and Mr Urpeth was the undertaker. Three old dears ran a small shop with hardly anything to sell, a Post Office, Co-op, Church Sexton, Mr Waterson the Tailor, a Butcher and farm hinds were all based along there. We had more facilities than the big villages have today.'

Staff and children in 1929 outside the school with its distinctive period leaded windows. Olde World but any would-be window cleaners nightmare.

## Widdrington Women's Institute

The WI was formed in 1923 and operates from a smart, compact village hall owned by the Institute and gives ladies from the area access to many activities ranging from adult education to charity work. It is also a centre for many meetings and events. A recent anniversary in June 2003 saw the ladies celebrate the 80th birthday of the WI which was well attended.

*Right*: The Institute's oldest member Hazel Johnson cuts the celebration cake made by Margaret Brown with the WI president Lynda Bell in attendance.

**The Hermit Of Warkworth**

The ladies of the manor have been described as fair of hair and light of eye, perhaps another indication of the families Anglo Saxon origins. The most famous and best loved member was Isabel as described in the legend of *The Hermit Of Warkworth.*

*Fair Widdrington the maiden's name*
*Yon towers her dwelling place*
*Her sire an old Northumbrian chief*
*Devoted to thy race*

Isabel lived up to her family's fighting tradition by asking her beloved Bertram of Bothal Castle to fame the helmet she had given him before they married.

*Young Bertram loved a beauteous maid*
*As fair as fair might be*
*The dewdrop on the lily's cheek*
*Was not so fair as she*

Bertram led a border raid with the Percys and Widdringtons but was sorely wounded in the skirmish. Isabel set out to nurse him back to health but was kidnapped by the Scots and taken to Hethpool Tower. Bertram's brother disguised as a Scot rescued her but when fleeing from College Glen Sir Bertram himself appeared and slew his brother mistaking him for the enemy and mortally wounded the lovely Isabel who had tried to ward off the blows.

It is said that the distraught Sir Bertram made a Hermitage on the banks of the Coquet and there spent the rest of his days in penitence. True or not it brings a little romance and sadness to this medieval ballad sung in the 15th and 16th centuries and penned by Bishop Thomas Percy in the 18th. A visit to the hermitage does show the figure of a lady in repose and a bull's head which is the Widdrington family crest, I wonder?.

The old Hermitage at Warkworth hidden under trees on the North bank of the river Coquet and accessible by guided boat trips from the South aspect.

### Canny Crack: The Bee Man

Robert Reed of Widdrington was born in the middle of the 18th century and died on the 28th March 1821. Described as a pedlar and bee master and a man of good honest crack. Awarded a prize from the Society of Arms and Commerce for bee management, he kept a large part of his stock at Widdrington. Famed throughout the County for farming out his hives on the heather moors, he would often be seen exhibiting his stock at markets such as Alnwick and Morpeth with a swarm of bees hanging from his hand.

### The Widdrington Witch

There lived in the village a strange old woman who was known as the old Witch or Crone of Widdrington. She was often seen leaving her home before dusk in the company of her black hound and not returning until the next day. She roamed the shore and dunes of Druridge Bay gathering mussels and driftwood. It is said that on one occasion while collecting mussels from the rocks she and her hound were caught by the tide and drowned.

Since that day in the late 19th century, the figure of a woman dressed in black and with a black hound at her heels has been seen at close quarters in the dunes before mysteriously vanishing into the sea frets that abound around that area. On one occasion not so long ago a man came upon an old lady on the beach at Blakemoor and conversed with her. She was dressed in a shabby old black dress of the Victorian period and spoke with a refined accent having with her a huge black hound at her heel. It was winter and no one else on the beach. The man continued his walk then turned to watch the woman farming driftwood. Her and the dog vanished before his eyes and all that was left was a tiny heap of old burnt kindling.

### Ghostly Grave Digger

Anyone who was buried in the Churchyard during the middle part of the 20th century may possibly have had their grave dug by John Robert Laidlaw. He was a tough little character with a sense of humour that endeared him to all he met and very much at home with a pick, shovel, spit and spade at the ready. John Robert had many strange and humorous encounters in the graveyard and here is one that he related to me many years ago.

A 1960s picture of John Robert Laidlaw with family and friends. Left to right: Margaret Robinson, May Robinson, John Robert, Ethel Laidlaw, Dot Laidlaw.

'Aa was diggin a grave one hot sunny day and was nearly at the bottom when aa stopped ti hav a smoke. Aa heard someone come alang and then silence. Aa stuck mi heed ower thi top and seen this wife with her back ti me arranging flowers on a grave.

'Aa said, "hoo yi gan on missus, nice day eh?" She got such a gliff seeing me covered in clay peeping ower the top, she screamed, hoyed the flowers up in the air and ran like hell for the gate.'

## Hares and hounds at Houndalee

Widdrington in 1768 and the land owned by Sir George Warren with fields numbered to correspond with the various tenants who are shown bottom right. It can be seen that the Houndalee farm area was then tenanted by Mr Fenwick, Mr Storey and Mr Johnson. After the Annett family tenancy in the late 19th century it is the early 20th that provides an insight into Houndalee as a working farm.

The main house at Houndalee farm shows the date 1817 inscribed in a stone above the front entrance. This area until the early 18th century was included in the confines of the old Widdrington Park. It was about here that James II slew two deer in the park when staying at Widdrington Castle on his way from Edinburgh to London in 1603 where he was to be crowned king which united the two countries of England and Scotland. The farm is shown on Sir George Warren's map of 1768 when the land was cleared of old trees.

Local knowledge suggests the name of the farm came from the running of the hounds which ran in the lee of Widdrington Castle, certainly there are pockets of land known as Low and High Dog Kennels to the North and this theory remains a strong possibility as fields, parcels of lands and farms were often named after people who were early tenants, peculiarities of certain fields, wild life that lived there or even the contours and situation of the land.

**Gwen Keen's memories**

My grandparents John and Sarah Wallace came to Houndalee in 1922 and tenanted the farm from Greencroft Estates. There were four children Kathleen, Jim, Mary and Ed. The lads took over the tenancy in 1961 while my mother Mary also lived at the farm with my dad Wilf Kelly and me. As well as the usual farming activities, grandma and mam made butter and kept hens, turkeys, and geese. My uncle Jim Wallace bred hunters and won many prizes at point to point racing and he rode the horse that pulled the hare smell for the coarsing around the Widdrington fields. He also cut a fine figure wearing his hunting outfit when riding with the local foxhounds.

Mam told me that there was a dummy airfield at the end of the mile road and the Home Guard were active there during the Second World War. Sometimes Captain Kirby slept in the back bedroom and his men occupied the granary. Two huge trees were chopped down at the end of the front drive as they were thought to be used by enemy aircraft as markers to bomb Acklington Aerodrome.

It was 1976 when the Wallace family retired from farming and left Houndalee to live in nearby Ellington.

John and Sarah Wallace who came to Houndalee from the Rothbury area in 1922.

Family group at the farm in the 1960s. Left to right: Ed Wallace, Mary Kelly, Jim Wallace and Wilf Kelly with pony Gypsy.

Farming was a family business and any extra income was a welcome boost to the tenants of any farm. Here is a picture of Sarah Ann Wallace feeding and handling her turkeys in the 1940s. They were corn fed and sold off for Xmas.

Jim Wallace a fine horseman shown here leading at a point to point meeting.

## Dririgge, Druiche Oaks and Druids

Druridge once a hamlet in the Parish of Woodhorn and covered in ancient times by the great forest of Chevington, lies in close proximity to the North Sea, the attendant sand dunes and superb beach which radiates North and South along a six mile stretch of coastline.

Druridge is a corruption of names that the area possessed at various periods over at least a thousand years. Druiche is one such spelling, Dririgge is another spelling which simply means dry hill. Another source states Ridge of Oaks and perhaps the most arguable, place of the Druids. While it would be easy to imagine on a wild and windy day in winter a Druids' meeting place or celebrating the Summer Solstice in June, no evidence has yet come to light.

An interesting mediaeval story states that a William Tascha contested the right of Sir Bertram de Widdrington to his estate and challenged him to a duel with his champion Alan of Dririg. Neither William or Alan turned up on the appointed day and the gallant Sir Bertram retained his lands

Druridge bay was in fair weather a haven providing anchorage for shipping that would unload and take on cargo here. Ships would bring in limestone from Durham to be burnt in kilns along the extensive dunes and the commodity used by the local farmers.

After the threat of a nuclear power station was averted and the cessation of sand extraction from the beach it appeared that this wild and wonderful place would be left in peace, and so it was until the outbreak of foot and mouth when the powers that be decided that the links would be used to burn livestock. Once again fires were lit and the air filled not with limestone but acrid smoke and stench of death.

The Scots Pines at Druridge Links replaced the ancient forest of Chevington but even they are feeling the affects of age and weather with few of the originals left standing in this fine picture.

This picture tells it all as the proposed nuclear power station is given the thumbs down by Druridge Bay campaign members and the public at a rally at Druridge Farm. Campaign member Bridget Gubbins stands at the cairn created over the years by not hundreds but thousands of folk who laid a stone in the hope that this would help to preserve this beautiful haven.

## Chibburn Priory and its Sermons in Stones

Low Chibburn Priory lies midway between Druridge Bay and Widdrington Village and is now a scheduled ancient monument. The Commandery was recorded in 1313 as the property of the Knights Templar and Knights Hospitallers created on military orders of St John of Jerusalem after the crusades to care for the sick and give refuge to pilgrims on their way to Lindisfarne.

After the dissolution of the monasteries in the 16th century Chibburn was granted to the Widdrington family and used as a Chapel and Dower House. During the second world war the slits in the Chapel wall were used as look out posts in event of an enemy invasion on the East Coast. The West side of the site was in reasonable condition until the 20th century and the house occupied by tenants up until 1940. A decision to opencast the area for coal in 1957, known as Radar North site, saw the mining operations surround the historical site and a total of 8 million tons of coal was produced over 16 years after which the land was returned to farming.

The Widdrington Dower House was a substantial building even in the 20th Century as seen in this old picture taken from the North West and lived in by estate and agricultural workers.

Part of the old Chapel now minus its roof but with outer walls still intact and attached to the Dower House in this photo from the late 19th century.

To capture the spirit of the early history often a visit is necessary and in this case a family walk to the Perceptory with a camera in hand. My youngest son and his three children stand in front of the old Chapel with the Dower House ruins to the rear.

# Ebb and Flow

The firm clean sand was an attraction to the Newcastle and District Motor Club as far back as the 1920s and they held many events there right up until the late 1950s. The races attracted entries from far and wide and many local riders like Tommy and John Reynolds competed here successfully. Naturally the races were subject to time and tide with Sunday well supported by the public who had a bird's eye view from the sand dunes.

*Right*: The Motor Clubs 1926 trials at the bay catered for classes from motorcycles to racing cars and net proceeds from programme sales were given to the Chevington Children's Distress Fund at a time of the miners' seven month dispute.

*Below*: Only a practice session for bike 61 and rider but on raceday the high backdrop of dunes served as a ready made grandstand for hundreds of spectators.

THE NEWCASTLE AND DISTRICT MOTOR CLUB.

TRAVERS

SPEED TRIALS

FOR THE

"NORTH MAIL" LIGHT CAR AND UNLIMITED SOLO CHAMPIONSHIP.

THURSDAY, JUNE 24TH,

1926, COMMENCING 5-30 P.M., AT

EAST CHEVINGTON SANDS,

NORTHUMBERLAND.

Under A.C.U. Open Permit for Motor-cycles, Side-Cars, and Three-wheeled Cycle Cars. R.A.C. Closed Permit No. 567, for Light Cars, Touring Cars, Single Seater and Racing Cars.

Under the General Competition Rules of the A.I.A.C.R. and the R.A.C. (Four-wheeled Cars), the International Competition Rules of the F.I.C.M., and the General Competition Rules of the A.C.U. (for Motor Cycles), and Supplementary Regulations.

Organised by the Newcastle and District Motor Club on behalf of the North-Eastern Centre A.C.U.

This is an A.C.U. Open Trial, and as such it must be run with every regard to the safety of the Public and Competitors. On the success of this Trial depends whether or not a Permit will be granted by the Autocycle Union next year, consequently is is up to the spectators to lend assistance and to KEEP WELL CLEAR OF THE TRACK. At the first sign of encroachment THE RACING WILL BE STOPPED.

PROGRAMMES - THREEPENCE.

The nett proceeds from the sale of these Programmes will be handed to the Chevington Children's Distress Fund.

Stewards (Red and White Rosettes):—
J. S. DAWSON, C. WEBB, T. STOREY, H. FOX, G. HEATH.
Judge: W. BAXTER (Purple Rosette).
Starter: GEO. W. RAPER (White Rosette).
Official Timekeeper: H. N. ELLIS, Liverpool (Yellow Rosette).
Chief Marshal: H. R. SHAW (Red Rosette).
Parking Marshall: GEO. BRADFORD (Blue Rosette).
Secretary of the Meeting and Clerk of the Course:
L. CHARLTON, 116 Pilgrim St., Newcastle (Blue & White Rosette).
Hon Treasurer; GEO. W. RAPER, 72 Northumberland Street, Newcastle.

An old stalwart of the races, Ted Hoy in typical pose easing his bike around the beach on a trial run.

Tom Reynolds, well known local rider, roars away from J. Taylor of Choppington who comes to grief on a corner after a thrilling duel at an event by the Newcastle Club in aid of the British Empire Cancer Campaign in the 1950s. Every supporter welcomed Tom and knew of his famous machine a 197cc Dot.

# SECTION TWO

# WIDDRINGTON COLLIERY

## THE VILLAGE THAT JUST DISAPPEARED

Widdrington Colliery Council School pupils almost a century ago.

This article penned by an unknown scribe in 1875 shows the impact of deep mining to the area.

Seven years ago a pit was sunk one and a half miles to the West of the old village which until then had been a purely agricultural area. Houses were built, a new population gathered and a new village formed which for size and importance far outstrips the ancient village of the Widdringtons.

Here as at Longhirst the houses of the men are of a very comfortable class although the first ones to be built are too small. The Pit Row has three types of house, one for officials and the other two for workers. Pantries are large and airy, each house has its own privy and ash pit and the men can have almost as much garden as they wish. The worst row in the place is Brickyard Row the houses of which have only two rooms and destitute of privies and ash pits.

Mr Cole of Bebside has recently been appointed manager of the Colliery and is somewhat of a sanitary reformer and the new houses which are being built since he took command are a great advance on the old ones. One new row of concrete houses are in progress each of which will have four rooms and a new brick row of the same size has also been commenced at the head of which a Mechanics' Institute is to stand.

There is a small Co-operative store in the village run from a dwelling house but Mr Cole has promised to build larger premises. As yet there are no Chapels in the place nor is there a school although both these needs are catered for in the old village. As the pit progresses so the need for more men and houses and where once there was little sign of human habitation there will soon be one of the most extensive Collieries in this part of the county which will soon swarm with sturdy miners.

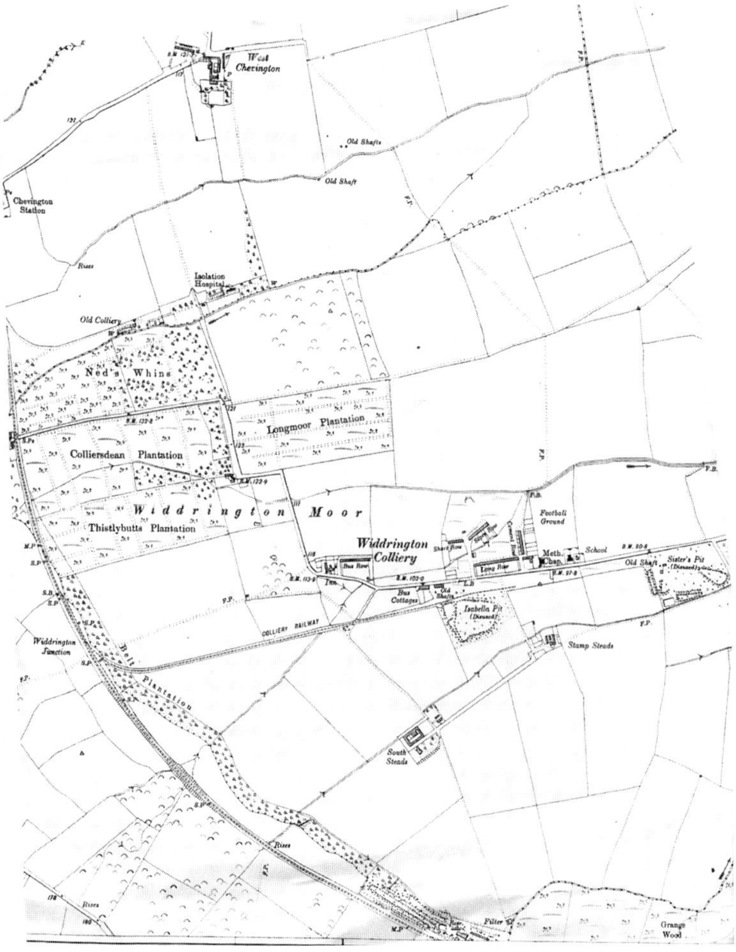


*Left*: A map of the Village in 1925 showing the rows of Long, Short, Store and Cement in relation to the new School, Chapel and the Colliery pits.

Long Row was aptly named with the most houses of all the streets in the Colliery Rows in this old postcard of 1905.

Short Row distinctive by the design of the houses and the first to be vacated in the exodus when the village was condemned.

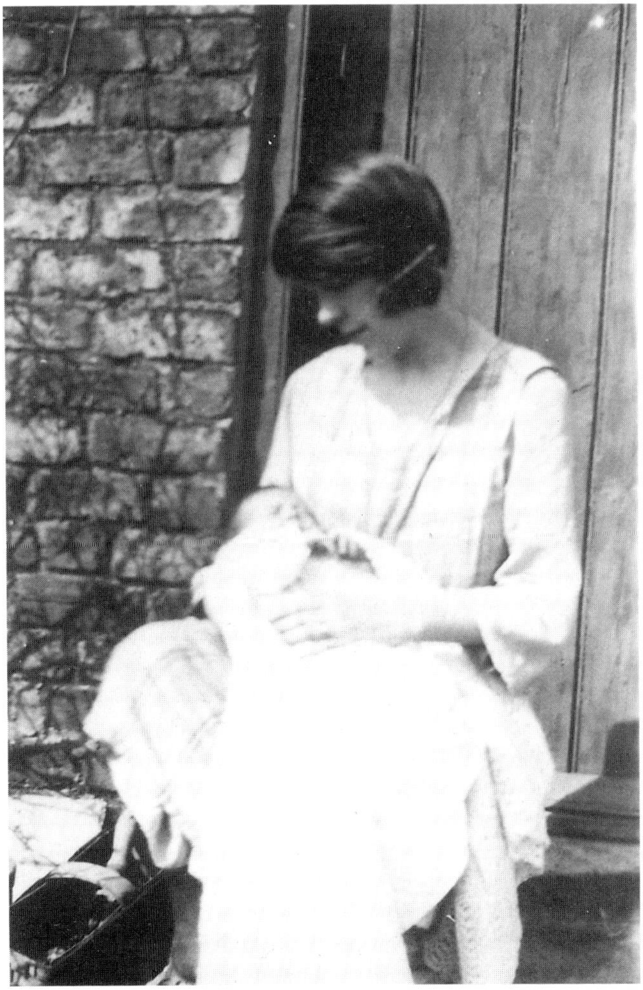

*Above*: Store Row, in 1905, the name thought to have come from the first Co-op in the village which operated from one of the houses there.

*Left*: Outside the back door of 10 Store Row and a wonderful snap of mother and daughter as Laura Harding cradles baby Elizabeth in her arms.

**Looking Back by Nancy Stewart (née Arthur)**

Our family lived in Cement Row during the 1920s and 30s and my dad worked at Ellington Colliery. The street got its name as its walls were filled with clinker and finished with a coat of cement unlike the other brick rows of Long, Store, Short and Bus. The walls were so hollow and thin it was hard to knock a nail in.

The Junction Inn where Mr Patterson and later Mr Doughty were tenants was named the Owld Bus as this is where we caught a horse and trap to Chevington Station and later the bus would turn here. Quoits were played behind the Inn and men came from far and near to win as the stake could be as high as £50 which was a fortune in those days of low wages. There was a store in the village and McKays, Anderson and Foggos ran shops from their homes and the Post Office was at the Station. The Institute was well used and concerts and dances were held here and I believe Mr French was one of the early Secretaries. Joe Davison was the milkman and we took out a pint jug which he filled from a churn. A strange sight was the appearance of a fish and chip van which was converted from an old hearse but that was no drawback cos the fish and chips were a real treat to us bairns once a week.

The toilets were middens across the lane and emptied by Tommy Smith into a horse drawn cart also used for delivering coal. Of course when we were taken on a yearly trip to Druridge Bay no one would venture into Tommy's cart for the smell and we all piled onto Hay Bogies.

We had a friendly little School where Mr Thompson was head and Mr Cook and Miss Clark were teachers. We often had school plays and concerts held in the Institute. There was a Methodist Chapel and the Hogg family were prominent members.

The colliers' coal concession was delivered by horse and cart, but this load is for an official with only the best coal used. The ordinary miner received small coals with lots of duff mixed in.

The Junction Inn or the Bus as it was known in 1912. In 1887 Ed Johnson is listed as tenant of the beer house at the Junction and surgeon Henry Hoy lived there. It looks like washing day Monday for the ladies of Bus Row behind and a good drying day as clothes can be seen sailing in the wind.

Bill Kell bought the pub in 1964, refurbished it over the years and sold out to Tetleys in 1986 and built a cottage next door. Here is the Junction as it was in 1964 sale.

*Right*: Improvements on the way in the 1970s in the top photo with a porch and new windows outside while inside Bill's father Old Kell serves at a refurbished and well stocked bar.

*Below*: During the 70s and 80s the Junction was the Country Pub to visit and take the young ones as it was one of the first to cater for family needs. Here it is much improved when Bill sold out in 1986.

**Clover and Birdsong by Isobel Bell**

I lived in Bus Row cottages at number 17 and round the corner from the Junction Inn. There were 18 houses built some way from the rest of the community. A tiny one up one down cottage and a long garden down to the main road which could only be reached by crossing a wooden bridge over a stream. The back street was cobbled and a standpipe in the middle of the street supplied the water which had to be carried in pails. This was a place where women met and gossiped while waiting their turn at the tap. My teacher was Miss Rankin at the Council School and in spring each child was asked to bring a penny to hear the birdman imitating the calls of wild birds. The field next to the School was full of wild flowers and clover and the hedges in May full of blossom.

*Above*: Quoits was played behind the Junction Inn a sport favoured by many colliers in the pit villages and Widdrington was no exception with the winner taking home as much as £50 in some of the big matches during the 1920s and 30s which was a fortune at that time during the depression years. Here are the Widdrington Quoiters in the 1920s posing for a photo at the Junction Inn. Man in the centre middle row is Jack Davison.

*Left*: A game in full swing in the 1920s and full concentration for the quoiter. The idea was to throw the quoit and ring the iron bar called a hob which was set in the ground surrounded by a bed of clay.

# Teaching the Young Folk

The first school in the Colliery was built and owned by the Widdrington Coal Company and known as a Public Elementary School. In 1887 the headmaster was W.J. Forster assisted by Phoebe Mawson, with a total of 160 mixed pupils 80 of these being infants. This School was actually part of the purpose built Mechanics' Institute until a new school was built in 1909 to accommodate 204 children with Eleanor Bell in charge of the infants. The new school which closed on the 26th October 1953 was then named Widdrington Council School.

The new Colliery School and Schoolhouse with teachers after the opening in 1909.

An early photo of Colliery pupils and teacher of class 6. The manner of dress suggests pre 1900 making this one of the oldest Colliery School photos available.

1908 and the School had its own management committee then, all male with a fine assortment of headwear including straw boaters, cloth caps and panamas all seen here at the School Treat.

These lads around ten years of age and members of the school cricket club are all holding an item connected with the sport. They would have the distinction of having attended both the old and the new School built in 1909.

Kitted out with sashes and supported by two lady teachers these young pupils are ready to face their opponents in a netball match at the new School. Annie Harding holds the ball and on her left is Laura Harding.

From the right Laura and Annie Harding with their friend show how the young girls dressed for school in the early part of the 20th century with long hair neatly tied back over a sensible, durable outfit with long stockings and sturdy shoes.

On to the 1920s and different aged youngsters in group 6 with a few names to add to these Colliery pupils. Back 4th left: Daisy Elliot, 7th Maisie Mckay with Mr Thompson the teacher. Middle row: Miss Rankin who features in Maurice Hilliard's book *The Years It Was Summer*, 3rd fourth and 5th left are the Arthur girls Mary Nancy and Peggy. John Robinson is second left in the front row.

The School produced a panto *Alice in Wonderland* in 1931, held in the Institute. Some of the youngsters from that year included, left to right, back row: Gladys Miller, Bob Scott, Tom Stansbury, Colin Bell, Joyce Foggo, Ruth Taylor. Front row: Millie Kell, Alec Morton, Dick Stansbury, Nancy Arthur, Sylvia Coates.

*Right*: Three young pupils at the schoolhouse were these smartly dressed lasses in 1926: Jean, Isobel, and Nellie Hogg who later joined the exodus to the new pit village of Lynemouth .

*Below*: The Methodist influence was soon in evidence and a Chapel was built in the village in 1894 serving the needs of a growing community. Here the Chapel can be seen and standing close by is the Mechanics' Institute which was also Widdrington's first education facility.

# The Tute!

The original Mechanics' Institute built by Widdrington Coal Company fell into disrepair after Widdrington Colliery closed and the Company turned its interests to the new Ferneybeds development. In 1924 Ashington Coal Company decided to take a hand as many of the Colliery Village residents then worked at Ellington, Linton, and Ashington collieries which were part of the Ashington Coal Company's group.

The Institute was reconstructed by its benefactors at a cost of £800 and formally re-opened by the Managing Director of the Ashington Coal Company Mr Ridley Warham on the 25th April 1925. In attendance were Mr Short President of the Institute, Bill Straker former Widdrington Colliery worker and Northumberland Miners' Secretary and Mr Colvin of Ellington Miners' Union. Mr Colvin said that it was a good thing for the Widdrington workmen to be taken over by the Ashington Coal Company. The new facilities included a hall with a stage, cloakrooms, library, billiard and games room, heating and kitchen.

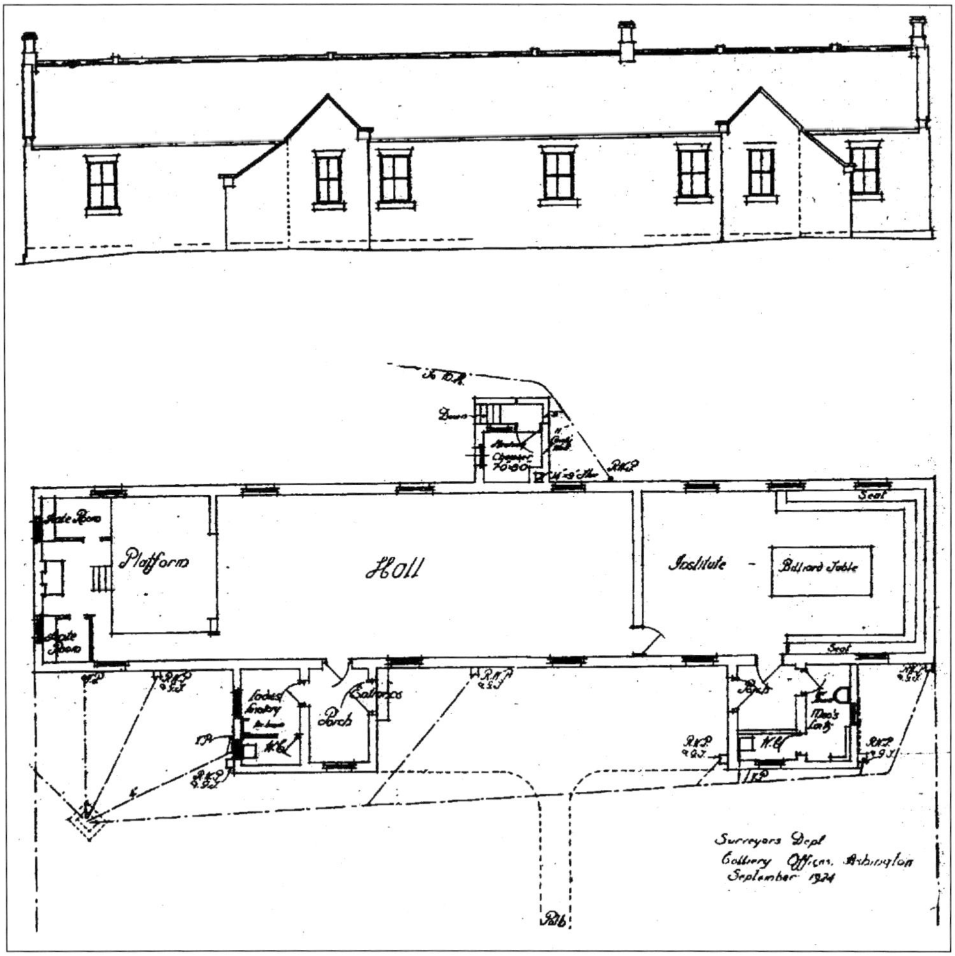


The reconstructed former Mechanics' Institute and school as designed by Ashington Coal Company in 1924.

## Shop at the Co-op

The old Co-op Store which started its life as a small house in the Colliery Rows in 1872 was well supported by the miners' wives. By 1880 a dividend on purchases of 2s 5d in the pound was made and had a membership of 138. The start of an annual tea for members was held and in 1884 200 villagers attended. By 1900 the divi had increased to 4s 3d in the pound and the membership stood at 297. The manager in 1887 was Mr Scott.

New premises were built in aptly named Store Row during the 1920s adding milk trading to their long standing Grocery, Drapery, Hardware, Furnishings, Shoe, Butchery, and Tailoring departments. By 1940 the Store was abandoned along with the Village as the Pit had closed long ago and the buildings condemned while the pitfolk moved on to more modern housing facilities in Widdrington Station and Lynemouth.

*Right*: Each branch had its set of rules and always a caption embracing the Co-op's affinity to the working classes and the poor folk of the Parish.

REG. NO. 1504 R.

RULES

OF THE

WIDDRINGTON

CO-OPERATIVE SOCIETY LIMITED.

*Established August 9th*, 1872.

*Registered Office :* WIDDRINGTON STATION, MORPETH.

These laws, though human, sprung from those Divine ;
Love laid the scheme, love guides the whole design.
To aid poor men—for them these laws were made,
Not to infringe upon the rights of trade.

ALL PURCHASES TO BE PAID FOR ON DELIVERY.

PELAW-ON-TYNE :
CO-OPERATIVE WHOLESALE SOCIETY'S PRINTING WORKS.
1927.

*All local Societies had their own set of rules "To aid poor men".*

The Co-op staff of the store at the end of Store Row or Co-op Terrace as some folks knew it, all well turned out and ready for business. Names known are Jimmy Smith on the left and Lizzie Adams in this picture of the early 1930s.

## William Straker CBE, JP

Bill Straker came to Widdrington Colliery shortly after the pit opened and worked there for 34 years. He soon developed a keen interest in trade unionism, the co-op movement, politics and religion which he retained for the rest of his life. He became secretary of the local branch of the miners' union and in 1908 agent of the Northumberland Miners' Association the same year as his appointment to the board of directors of the Newcastle branch of the Co-op Printing Society. Becoming the miners' corresponding secretary, he later succeeded Thomas Burt as general secretary of the County Miners' Union. He retired from this post in 1935 aged 80 years.

Bill was still active on many fronts in 1939 at the tender age of 84 being a life governor of the Royal Victoria Infirmary, Chairman of the Northumberland Aged Miners' Homes Association, a member of the County Education Committee and a magistrate. For the most part a self taught man a Primitive Methodist and tee totaller who began his union activities fighting for the Widdrington Colliery miners' rights and believed in conciliation as opposed to strike action he attained much throughout his career which spanned the bitter feuds of Coal Owners and pitmen during the latter part of the 19th century until the coal strikes and recession years of the 1920s and 30s.

William Straker during his time as Northumberland Miners' General Secretary. Bill died on the 31st December 1941 aged 86 years.

## Put onto the Street

It was never easy to be a union man fighting for miners' rights in the early years as the Redpath Family found to their cost when they were evicted by Ashington Coal Company in 1932. The family was split and father Ogle and two sons John and Freddie went to live at Stobswood. Ogle had been working at Ellington Colliery and after a while he was taken on at Stobswood by manager Mr Spence. A further dispute some years later saw Ogle suspended from his work but was later re-instated by James Bowman.

During his suspension the family had no coal for heating and no food. Neighbours brought them goods including meat and fruit. One kind fellow brought a chicken and later it was discovered the Pit Manager's hen house had been raided.

## Flying Snaggies

Arnott Hope remembers: 'I worked at Halls farm and used to fill the milk churns with the water from Stampy Steads which was softer than anywhere else. I can remember taking milk down to the school when the soup kitchens were on in the 1920s. One day in the field near to the pit shaft all the turnips had been hoyed into the air from the force of the underground coal blasting. There were turnips everywhere, aye lad flying turnips.

Adam Laidler had a horse and cart, he was a real character and could get you anything you wanted, anytime. There was always lads running around helping him. The first bus was really just a Ford Wagon with two benches. Then Rennisons had a bus and it went on fire one day and folk were crawling out the windows. Then Ramsey and Dowse ran buses after that. Oliver was the Polis and lived in Bus Cottages.'

## War Hero Honoured

On September 16th 1918 Sergeant Coates of Widdrington Colliery who had won the Military Medal fighting in France was honoured by a large gathering who met in the Mechanics' Institute. Mr English manager of Ferneybeds Colliery presented Sgt Coates with a gold watch saying it was a pleasure to honour one of their own boys.

## Remember Me

Elizabeth Harding never forgot the boys of the Colliery who had gone to fight in the Second World War and helped those who had been taken prisoner and settled in the German Prison Camps in the only way she could. Food parcels as many as were allowed were sent abroad and gratefully received by many local POWs.

William James Smith of Widdrington seen here back left was prisoner No 18999 at Stalag 1XC when he sent this postcard to Mrs Harding of Store Row in 1943 after receiving a food parcel.

# The Two Pits

There were two pits at Widdrington, the first the Isabella sunk in 1868 and abandoned in 1890. The second named the Sisters to the East of the village. It is mooted that the name Sisters referred to the third Lord Widdrington's seven daughters and his Lordship is reputed to have planted seven trees in the vicinity of his castle in their honour but other schools of thought suggest that it simply means two sister pits. However the name of one of Lord Widdrington's daughters famed in the old ballad *The Hermit Of Warkworth* was named Isabell which certainly gives food for thought.

The owners were Widdrington Coal Company. From the onset of coal production the Yard, Five Quarter and Main seams were proving difficult to work, more so those sited at the West Incline on the North Side and accidents were a common occurrence. Between 1871 and 1898 there were 11 deaths at the Colliery. The first recorded was Tom Anderson on the 26th June 1871 a labourer caught in an engine flywheel and on 5th November 1898 George Spowart died in a fall of stone. These are just some of the ones known, there may have been many more whose lives were taken winning the prized black diamonds. In 1887 there were 260 men and boys employed at the pit, the Manager was James Hay and the Engineer Robert Lee.

The Manager in 1890 was James Hay Jnr with James Durey as his Under Manager and the colliers numbers reduced to 212 men. The land was leased to the Coal Company by Thomas Taylor and Earl Grey. By 1909 the owner Colonel Lambert was trading under the name of Vernon West Hartley-Widdrington Hartley Steam Coals. In 1910 the Manager was John Rogers and his understudy George Turner.

By 1920 the pit was run down, then in 1923 Widdrington Coal Company went into liquidation.

Old Widdrington Colliery Screening Plant at the Sisters Site around 1900 with a set of tubs on the bridge landing and coal wagons being loaded underneath. The pit chimney at the rear was demolished in the 1920s.

Two young collier lads in typical pit attire about 1900 breaking in a pit pony to harness and coal tub on the surface prior to being sent underground to work.

The collier's lot was never easy and confrontation with owners on wages and conditions was always ongoing. The strike of 1912 saw the locals scrounging fuel for the home fire from the pit heaps. Coal that they themselves had already dug from the pit and cast aside as waste.

## Sport and Pastimes

A thriving pit village community did not take long to organise its leisure time groups and sporting activities. Football was played before the 20th century and a team operated in the 1920s and 30s. Cricket was well supported with a fine pitch at the south east of the Colliery. Henry Annett and Ogle Redpath were involved with organising. Ogle has the distinction of taking a hat-trick of wickets against a County side and his photo hangs in the Jesmond club house.

Cock fighting was held in a pit just opposite the Junction Inn and the spectators mound can still be seen today. Dick Stamp was a key figure and kept many champion cocks. Totally illegal, colliers would wager big money on the outcome of these contests. Quoits had a large following behind the Junction Inn and a substantial kitty for the winner. Bill Kell found old Quoits there when renovating the pub in the late 1960s.

When the Institute was built a billiards room was included and a reading room for the miners. During the depression years of the 1920s and 30s Hare Coursing was popular with the workers who had more time on their hands albeit with little money in the back pocket. The Vernon Arms was the venue for meeting and celebrations.

Taken outside the Junction Inn in 1908 this Colliery team could not muster a full set of strips to play in. Wages were poor for the early miners and football kit was way down the list in terms of necessities.

Widdrington Utd, 1919-20. Time marches on and now this fine Widdrington team who won the North Northumberland league title in 1920 have a new white strip to play in. Little did they know that the following year would see a bitter 13 week coal strike that would see many Widdrington families accepting food from soup kitchens.

Moving on to the 1920s and more names to this side and their committee. Note the real leather ball they played with in the old days. Included back row: Ernie White, Jack Davison, Bob Arthur, Jack Mclean, Bob Short, Billy Moore. Middle row: John Wardhaugh, John Grainger, Eddy Wardhaugh. Front row: Louis Proudlock, John Kelly.

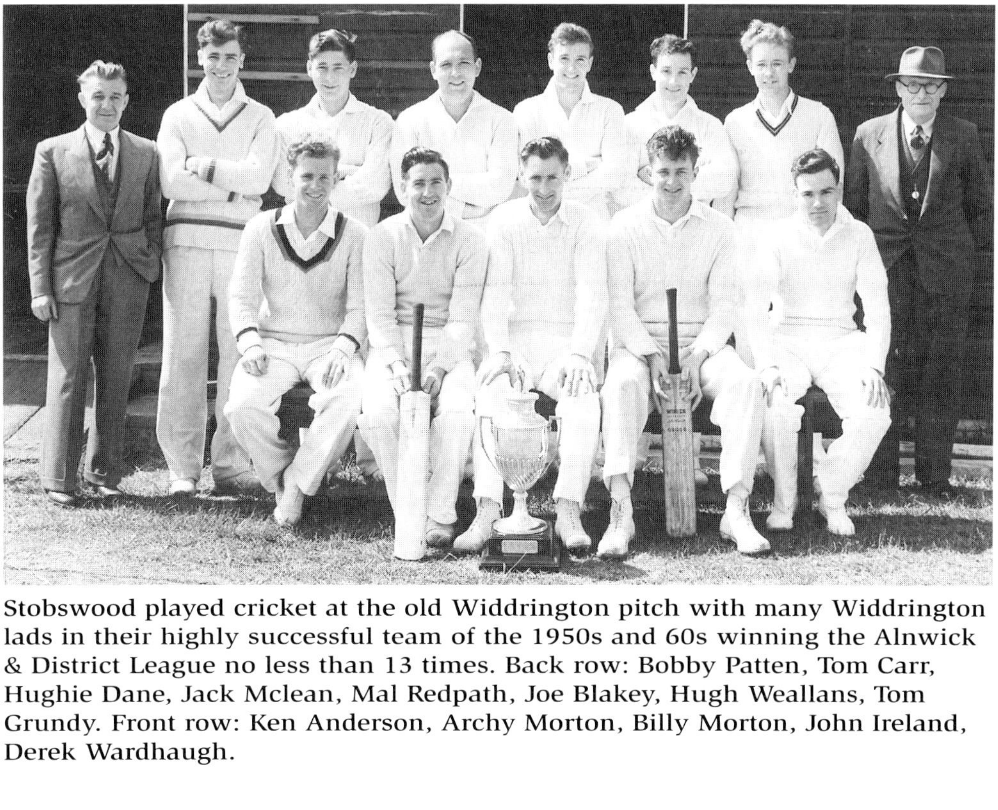

Stobswood played cricket at the old Widdrington pitch with many Widdrington lads in their highly successful team of the 1950s and 60s winning the Alnwick & District League no less than 13 times. Back row: Bobby Patten, Tom Carr, Hughie Dane, Jack Mclean, Mal Redpath, Joe Blakey, Hugh Weallans, Tom Grundy. Front row: Ken Anderson, Archy Morton, Billy Morton, John Ireland, Derek Wardhaugh.

## A Place in Paradise by Annie Dodds McInnes

My dad John Dodds was head woodsman for Thomas Taylor of Chipchase who owned the Widdrington estate. Our family lived in a cottage just west of Widdrington Colliery which was where I attended school. The parcel of land about here was called Paradise and so it was to us children in a quiet rural retreat. Mr Stockdale the estate gamekeeper lived in the cottage next door and I remember the shooting parties he led for Mr Taylor and his guests around the 1920s. To supplement my dad's meagre wage we kept hens and grunters and a cow named Polly which my mam Elizabeth milked every day. Along the track from us lived Tommy Smith in the Lodge House at the entrance to the little tin isolation hospital and we took milk there to be used for the patients. Tommy would bring the patients in his horse and trap from the outlying villages who were suffering from smallpox, scarlet fever and other infectious diseases.

Aunt Meg lived at the Colliery and sold sweets from her house and I can recall one day at school when all the pupils were taken out to watch the pit chimney being blown down as the mine had been closed for some years. The only transport those early days was horse and trap for folks that wanted to go to Widdrington Station or to Chevington where we caught the train to Amble on feast days. Sadly when dad died in 1926 we had to move from our little piece of Paradise to a new life at the new housing estate at Widdrington Station where I settled and still live at the time of writing.

Editor: Medical Officers Health reports from late 19th century to the 1920s show urgent schemes needed for sewage and waste disposal at Widdrington. In 1913 there were 110 cases of infectious diseases reported in Morpeth area.

Annie Hope: 'I worked as Cook at the old isolation hospital during the Second World War after it was taken over by the Land Army girls who worked for the local farmers. It looked like an old army hut converted into a hospital. The girls needed a good meal after being out working in the fields all day.'

## Girl Ghost Of Stamp Steads

The tiny little parcel of land with farm house and cottages that lay to the south west of the Colliery was known as Stampy Steads and the Stamp family are known to have lived here and at South Steads in the 19th century. From there comes a most curious tale of sadness and haunting. A young girl who lived in one of the cottages had a dog which she loved dearly. Every morning and evening she would run through the fields with her companion at her heels.

One late October day after school with dusk approaching she raced along the rutted track and up onto the pit heap of the Isabella Colliery with her faithful hound alongside her. Feeling the wind on her back she went faster and faster until her feet barely touched the black shale of the tip. Whooping and hollering with sheer pleasure she never did see the end of the slag heap as the wind strengthened to gale force and carried her and the dog to their death over the edge and into the depths of the quarry below. Sad indeed when her family found the girl and the dog side by side in the darkness. But what is most curious is the fact that no sign of injury was ever found on their bodies. Both looked at peace merely sleeping they said.

One year later to the very day a man out walking at dusk saw a girl and a dog racing along the pit heap and disappear over the edge into the darkness. Many sightings were recorded over the following years always at dusk, some folk said the spectre whooped and hollered and the dog howled as if in warning. Other reports state the figure wailed like a banshee always appearing in the same place. A strange event occurred the year the pit heap was flattened when a local woman was returning to Stampy Steads. She saw a young girl in a white dress, a dog at her side running back and forth in the spot where the heap had been. On this occasion the lady came close to the girl who seemed in much distress. She noticed the girl's long straw coloured hair set in ringlets her piercing blue eyes and sharp features, and a distinctive strawberry scar on her neck. Tears flowed down her cheeks and she beckoned the woman before suddenly disappearing.

The description the lady gave of the girl matched exactly with that of the one the family supplied of their loved one who had set out those many years ago with her beloved dog to wander the fields of Stampy Steads.

## Memories

*Above*: The new Cement Row. Built in 1875 and fitted with mains electric in 1939 although classed as condemned houses the row provided housing for families waiting to take up tenancy at Widdrington Station and Lynemouth prior to and after the Second World War.

*Right*: A typical Collier lad around 1900 when times were hard down the pit. What a wonderful face full of joy and character in times of adversity. Boys like this would be working at least 12 hours underground and more if required.

## The Owld Sment Raa by F.E.D (Pompey 1947)

Editor: This poem given to me and edited to fit the book is obviously from an ex Colliery resident who had many happy memories of the village and its pit families.

The Lang Raa the Bus Raa the Short and the Store Raa
Are crumbled in the dust and exist no more
Noo your roofs are leaking your window panes have gone
A sorry sight you now must be and sad to gaze upon
The plasters peeling from your walls ceiling full of cracks
And smoke naa longer passes up your chimney stacks
The little bairns in tha beds are drenched wi winter rains
Mothers suffer from the draughts and dread rheumatic pains
Pantry walls are dripping the netties tumbling down
And noo the MOs on your back your tale of woes to crown.

Remember when we played ball at Wilson's corner end
How many evenings playing cards in Telfers did we spend
Winter nights and Tic-Tac drumming on Dixon's door
Many an owld wive's poss tub we scattered on the floor
Joe Wedderburn the buzzer man lived at number eight
He blew the buzzer right on time and often we were late
Owld Foster he would whack us and so would Mr Tait
For piddling neath his window or swingin on his gate
Tri-ball-the-rollies we played and cricket on the green
And many a bloody fight was added to the scene

Bill Straker was the union man and lived at number nine
He got the pitmen gardens and sure they kept them fine
Browns and Halls and Taylors and Arthurs there did dwell
Spowarts Trench and Adamsons that I remember well
The quoiters had their clay ends Bill Calder was the king
He never failed to find the hob in the middle of the ring
At pigeon racing on Saturday you would hear Bill Kelly shout
Bobs got one and Bills got one and aave got bloody nowt
Owld Charlton had a horse by the name of young crusty Jack
We chased him in the paddock field and jumped up on his back

Foggos had a shop where we went pay Friday nights
To spend our weekly happenies on liquorice delights
Tom Miller's show came every year and Lucy was the rage
With Alf and Tom on high wire and Clinker on the stage
Night Shift men trudge down the road Ned Urwin's the Master Shifter
Owld Tappers calling Martha home how often we have gliffed her
There's many a lass aave kissed and many a heart aave broken
Tales aave towld and words aave said I never should have spoken
But Dear owld Sment Raa the end it was bound to come
Yet nee matter what you'll always be home to some.

## SECTION THREE

# WIDDRINGTON STATION & FERNEYBEDS

Widdrington Station House and platform in 1905 showing the crossing with wooden gates and the signal cabin then on the North side. The Station Master in 1897 was recorded as Mr Matthew Hall. Records in 1910 show that the Station Master was Joseph Hutton Allan and then in the 1950s Mr J.W. Brimer was in charge of the station with Mr L. Dobie as signalman.

## The Rail Link

In January 1845 the Newcastle and Berwick Railway advertised for supplies of iron rails, rail-chairs and wood sleepers to be delivered at the eight ports of Newcastle, Blyth, Warkworth, Alnmouth, Beadnell, North Sunderland, Warren and Berwick.

This meant that track laying could be done simultaneously at many sites. It would have taken a vast army of navvies and horses and carts to fulfil this project. The track for Widdrington was shipped in via Amble and the railway was opened to the public on the 1st of July 1847. The local economy would have boomed at this time. Now Widdrington had a main line stop with a road level crossing with wooden gates, a fine Station House and passenger facilities. The ease of transport to the various ports in the region would have been a major factor in the decision of Widdrington Coal Company and Stobswood to sink their pits in the immediate area on the east side of the railway. Extensive coal reserves had been identified under the major part of the Widdrington Estate.

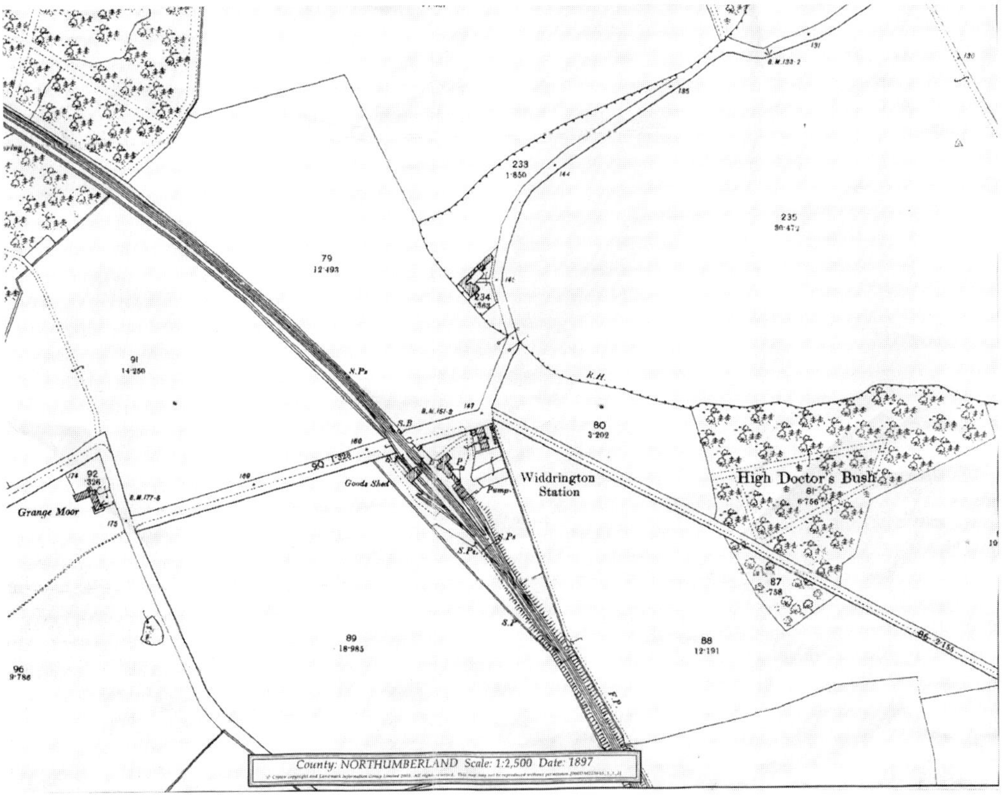


As shown on the map of the area from 1897 there were few houses save for the outlying farms and Station House here at this time.

A fine 1920s picture of Widdrington Station with Station Master Tom Bell with daughter Edie, a porter, passengers and a shy little lass just making the group on the right.

Times, signal boxes and trains all have changed in this picture with the signal box now on the South side of the crossing and the engine now diesel. Today the box has vanished, no longer needed in this hi-tech age.

## No names just Blocks by Betty Dodds

It was 1926 before people first tenanted the 42 Council Houses. They had no names at first, Mary Street was known as Block one and so on until they were christened with real names. Among the first tenants were the Dodds, Browns, Telfers, Carruthers and Smiths. Eventually a new estate was created and many folk from Old Widdrington Colliery moved here. The first GP that I remember was Dr Hunter from the Colliery who was carried on his rounds by horse and cart driven by Barry Queen. Then Dr Welch came. You always knew when he was about cos he smoked a pipe and had a lovely smell of St Bruno baccy about him. Old Dr O'Driscoll came in 1938 and now there is his son Finbar. Dick Oliver was the polis in the 1930s, then Mr Ireland and a fella called Scott came later. One thing that sticks in my mind is when Princess Royal visited her regiment during the Second World War when they were billeted in houses in Grange View.

There was no school, Stobswood being the nearest and no Co-op until a small branch opened in 1927. The first Church was the Roman Catholic in Grange Road in 1937. Then came St Mary's Church Hall in 1938 and the Methodists also had a Chapel built along Grange Road in 1958.

Recorded living in the area in 1938 were George Hindmarsh, a Haulage Contractor of Edith Street, Lance Queen, a Music Teacher, Flora McDonald who was the District Nurse from Ferneybeds, A&J Willoughby of the Gables.

*Above*: Widdrington Station's first Council Houses known as blocks before being christened with girls' names.

*Left*: Games were always played in the back streets and many a window fell to a cricket or football. When this happened the street was deserted in seconds. Here we have Alec Wallace at the wicket with young Jack Dodds as keeper in this snap taken in the 1930s at Mary Street.

## St Joseph's RC Church

The first Church was built in 1937 at Grange Road on land donated by the local GP, Doctor Welsh. It was simply two garages that were joined together by Mick Reilly and his friends. It served the local Catholic community well as it stood the test of time until it was pulled down and a new Church built in 1964 in the same position. The new pre-fabricated Church still serves the needs of the local community at the present time.

Kath Hyslop remembers: 'While our new Church was being built we held Mass in Widdrington Club. The committee were good to us they never charged us a penny.'

Local priest in the 1960s was the much respected Father O'Docherty seen here at the Church entrance with Widdrington lass Norma Scullion.

The new St Joseph's Church in 1967 and confirmation day for young Carmel Scullion. Included in this group are Peter Docherty and three of the Sanderson youngsters with the nun at the back who travelled from Alnwick on a Saturday to provide religious instruction.

## St Mary's Church Hall

The new Church replaced the old Stobswood Mission Church and building started in 1937 on land given by Stobswood Coal Company. Thomas Taylor donated £100 as did Mr Burn the colliery owner who also supplied the bricks. A foundation stone was laid on August 20th 1938 by Miss B.K. Burn who received a solid silver Eversharp Pencil suitably inscribed to mark the event.

### Penny a brick

The local people helped raise funds to build the Church by sponsorship of a penny a brick which was collected by Mary Kelly. The hall was well used and it could be partitioned off for various activities. There was a Youth Section, a choir and Sunday School with confirmation classes. Concerts and dances were a feature to help in the upkeep of the hall. Sadly it fell into decline, with fewer supporters and more maintenance required its demise came in 1980s when it was demolished.

This aerial picture shows how the Church which is the white building centre right was conveniently placed to serve the communities of Widdrington and Stobswood.

This 1940s snap was taken in the Church grounds and appears to show a group of young folk who took part in a play or Pantomime. Third from the right in the back row is Ernie Black.

*Above*: Margaret Routledge formed a dance class at the Church and here are three of her smart young pupils on stage in the early 1950s. Left to right: Pat Nichol, Maureen Lane, Norma Richardson.

*Right*: Two young star performers on stage at the Church Hall in this wonderful picture of 50 years ago are Norma Richardson on the left and Gwen Davidson posing in continental dress.

# Widdrington Methodist Chapel

It was 1953 when land was acquired along Grange Road by the Methodists and a building fund started the following year headed by Mr J.W. Brimer with a view to building a new Chapel to replace the old Stobswood Chapel and maintain the Methodist element of faith in the area. The local community were able to buy a brick for sixpence and this was a major source of income to pay for a new Church. In addition the J. Arthur Rank Trust gave £1,500, the Chapel Department promised £300 and Alderman Nixon £500.

A stonelaying ceremony was held on 31st May 1958 with stones laid by Rev John G. Lane, Chairman of Newcastle & District Methodists and by the oldest Chapel Member and local preacher George Bertram.

The new red brick Chapel was opened on 4th October 1958 by Mrs Daly of Blyth, wife of the architect and designer. The bus loads of Methodists from other areas who attended could not all be accommodated in the new Chapel and the ceremony was relayed to the overflow in the adjoining schoolroom. A celebration tea was held in St Mary's Hall at 3.30 pm for the then princely sum of one shilling and sixpence.

Built on a solid foundation of endeavour and faith the demise of the Chapel came in 1996 when the building foundations proved to be unsound causing serious problems in the structure which was demolished in 1996.

The Methodists still worship in the village with services at the Community Centre.

The Chapel as it was at the opening. A steady congregation of 31 souls, Sisterhood, Christian Fellowship, Sunday School and a Children's Night, it seemed to bode well for the following years.

The 25th Anniversary of the Chapel was celebrated with a tea in 1983 with a cake cut by Ina Clark the oldest member on the right attended by the Chapel secretary Mrs Brown.

## Shops about the place by Tommy Brown

My grandparents Jack and Isabella Hall ran a general dealers shop in Stobswood before the one on Grange Road. My mother later ran the Post Office from the house in Grange Road and prior to this from 1, Ena Street. At the Station the Store had a butchery department, grocery, drapery and hardware and above the main building was a hall where once the Parish Council would hold meetings and was used as a picturehall and well supported during the 1940s and 50s.

Edith Morgan: 'My dad Bert Queen was projectionist at the Co-op Hall Cinema. There was four different films a week and the prices were sixpence, ninepence, a shilling and one and six. Any trouble and there were two chuckers out, Louis Proudlock and Dick Wallace.'

Ladies of Widdrington Co-op staff in 1960 with the old fashioned delivery van that had only just superseded horse drawn delivery carts. From the left: Lorna Reed, Joyce Cowans, Audrey James, Janice Burns, Edith Queen, Joan Elliott, June Grainger and Betty Wardhaugh.

Widdrington Station Co-op premises in the 1980s, a fine building which was also home to many of the area's social activities. The shop bottom right of picture is the Widdrington Fish Shop.

## The Station Club

The first Social Club at the Station was a wooden hut in the 1920s and managed by Mr Boll. When the new Club was built it was the focal centre for many of the village social activities.

Bob Weddell: 'The Club was a base for the Stobswood Homing Society from at least the 1950s until the Society folded in 1991. We ran a weekly forecast and kept our pigeon clocks here.'

John Elliot: 'There was a well supported Leek Club here and at Xmas we held a big draw and there were turkeys, geese and cock chickens, bottles of spirits and lots of other prizes well worth winning.'

*Right*: The new Club as it was shortly after it opened, with three local patrons outside. Note the freshly painted fence at the path entrance and the shrubs surrounding. The men are Bill (Soldier) Redpath, Ogle Redpath, Pete Mavin.

*Below*: The Club was used as a base for a St John First Aid Class prior to the Second World War and well supported by local people. Included in the back row: Mr Scott, Robert Tweddell, Mr Weddell and Police Constable Weddell. Included in the front row are: Jack James, Matt James, Mr Storey, John Elliott and Mr J Elliott. The man in the background is Mr Henderson.

Every large organisation needs a working committee to oversee its affairs and Widdrington was no exception with an abundance of local talent. These are the men who formed the Committee in the 1950s. Included from the back are: Bill Murray, W. Bolton, Norman Scott, Jack Burge, Bob Redpath, Jim Farrell, Harry Todd, Bill Chirnside, Jack Wharton Ron Wanless, J. Potts, Joe Hagan.

Lots of local folk here in this late 1950s picture of Stobswood Juniors soccer side at Widdrington Social Club. Included back, left to right: Eric Wharton, Raphy Aspey, Malcolm Allan, Peter Angus. Front row: Tommy Gowland, Ronnie Warwick, Peter Gowland, Tom Walton, George Allen, John Oliver.

Disaster in June 1969 when the Social Club caught fire and everyone's imagination when the mile road was closed to allow the firemen to tackle the blaze and caught on film by Gordon Willoughby.

Adjoining the old Club is Widdrington's Training and Activity Centre, one of the important cogs in the wheel of the areas regeneration scheme which on this occasion is benefiting from a cheque from RJB Mining.

Margaret Jane Nicholson was 95 when she laid her last wreath for the Widdrington and Stobswood women's branch of the British Legion. She is seen here in the centre after receiving an award for being the longest serving member ever. Presenting the award were Morpeth Borough Council's Mayor and Mayoress Mr and Mrs Lough of Ulgham.

1977 saw celebrations countrywide for the Queen's Silver Jubilee and Widdrington & Stobswood organised a float to ferry their local youngsters to join in the Morpeth festivities. Pictured with hard hats and overalls in sympathy with their village's industrial heritage they are shown here aboard their transport at Morpeth.

Louise Currie of Energi is pictured back centre and headed this progressive group of residents who formed a Park Committee to the completion of the Park seen here at the opening ceremony in September 2003.

Much respected local MP Alan Beith and Morpeth Mayor Derek Thompson ready to cut the tape and declare the Park open watched by Widdrington youngsters.

## Time Will Tell

Two years ago sculptor Karl Fisher of Sunderland was commissioned to design an entrance to the new Park Complex and after much research into the area's history came up with the novel idea of a Widdhenge type structure based on time. After much hard graft sculpting the 12 huge blocks at Hadston Farm they were finally placed at the Park entrance in the summer of 2004. Each stone skilfully honed shows a piece of the Widdrington area's history from its castles to coal mines and is a unique structure that is governed by the sun and will face the test of time.

*Above*: Sculptor Karl Fisher stands with his back to the sun on the central dial in the middle of the circle which is inscribed with the months of the year and watches his shadow fall on one of the numbers set around the circle which gives the time of day at that moment.

*Left*: The theory of time is being put to the test and here are four of my grandchildren, pictured at the stones, ready to try it out for themselves.

## Bob Weddell on Duckets and Doos

The first pigeon men I knew in the area were at Stobswood where they had allotments long before they came to Widdrington. My dad and me moved our ducket from there in the 1950s to the site at Widdrington where the Park is today. Originally the members flew their birds in the Wansbeck Federation but then we foined the Coquetdale Federation and were known as Stobswood Homing Society.

The Club had a box van by the railway and that is where we kept our racing baskets and ring marked our birds for the races. Later we had to vacate the land as it was owned by the railways and they took it over. So we moved our hut to where the old folks home is now. Sad to say as often happens in the sport an arson attack destroyed the premises and all our racing baskets. The Federation rallied round and supplied us with baskets to keep the club going.

Being close to the railway had its benefits as we sent our birds training and racing by this means of transport. When the railways stopped taking pigeons we sent our birds by road transporter and ringed them at a wooden hut at Widdrington Club.

You had to be dedicated to be a pigeon man, they had to be exercised, trained, fed and watered and tended to every day of the year. Long races from the continent meant the birds were basketed on Thursdays for a Saturday race and if weather was bad it might be Monday before they were released to fly the 500 miles home. Often I have been at the ducket at 10 pm waiting for a race bird and my wife would bring my supper over on a summer night, I stayed until 11 pm when the race closed during darkness hours then opened again early next morning. It was possible to spend almost a whole weekend at the ducket waiting for the birds to home and if one did and won a good position in the race it could mean winning a fair bit money and make the whole year's work worthwhile.

Derek Foggo was our secretary and the club in the later years had fanciers from Lynemouth and Cresswell which helped to keep the club going when the membership decreased. There is no pigeon club now the young folk are not interested, they live a different life to the one we knew. The allotments by the railway line have gone and in their place a play park for the youngsters, Widdrington is expanding with fancy new houses, nowt stops the same does it.

DIY was the name of the game in the old days with little money available and Ned Davison an old Stobswood stalwart is pictured here in front of his beautifully constructed pigeon ducket which he built himself.

## The Model Master

Widdrington man Gordon Willoughby is well known for his ability to turn parts of old cookers and washing machines into models of almost anything. A hobby that started in 1980 has seen him produce countless models, some of which record the area's history with models of the Widdrington Co-op and the old Widdrington Arms Hotel.

All of his creations are fashioned using only a small bench, hammers, pliers and his bare hands. One feature of his early models for anyone who looks closely they will see his Scottie dog Mac who appears in them all.

Gordon, a retired Mechanic, drove tanks in the Second World War with the Armoured Brigade and after the D-Day landings was in action in France, Belgium, Germany and Denmark before seeing service in India where he was hospitalised for two years. He remembers that well and the Sunderland Flying Boat that brought him back home is now brought back to life in one of his models.

Gordon and his little helper Susan at a model rally at Woodhorn Colliery Museum with just a selection of his work. All of his models work with the aid of a battery, electrics, and the push of a button.

## Bullets, Bombs and Beaufighters

Stobswood and Widdrington like most other villages during the Second World War had its own Dads Army with a fair number of Officers who had served their country in the Great War. Facilities were made available at Widdrington Co-op to house a fire service and troops were stationed in houses in Grange View.

During the conflict a Beaufighter aircraft crashed at Stobswood killing the pilot and navigator and a land mine dropped at East Stobswood. A number of servicemen were brought back from war service during the Second World War to their former jobs at the brickyard which was considered vital to the Country's needs to assist the war effort.

One local lad Alf Foster served with 5th Platoon 7th/9th Royal Scots. Alf is pictured here first left in the second front row.

John Redpath: 'Our headquarters was the Benevolent Hall at Stobswood which was where we stored our guns. We trained around the area behind the pit heap and at Druridge Bay with regular soldiers who were billeted there and practised a mock invasion. I was the mortar man and what a gun that was. I shot at targets 400 yards away and the wind would take the shell way off its mark and adjustments had to be made all the time. My dad who had fought in the First World War headed a special team who had a secret cache of arms and equipment in a wood by the pit heap. The idea was if the country was overthrown then they would fight a guerilla war to the bitter end. These units were in place all along the East Coast with film actor Anthony Quayle mooted as the Chief.'

Mortar Man John Redpath sets his sights on target with his mortar crew close at hand to assist, including Jimmy Hulson, Ray Sandgren, Jack Mclean, Billy Shell.

A strong contingent of Stobswood and Widdrington Home Guard in 1943 with many of these men working at the pit or brickyard at that time to fuel the war effort and after a hard shift underground volunteer to drill and exercise for the sake of their country and their own little bit of England.

All over now and time to move on is the theme as Widdrington and Stobswood folk celebrate the end of the Second World War in 1945 in the field next to Dr O'Driscoll's house behind St Mary's Church. Races for the children were held and each one received an orange. Young girl front right is Irene Dunn who supplied the photo.

## Ball Games

Football and Cricket facilities have been shared throughout the years in the villages. First it was old Widdrington Colliery who had the base for the first soccer and cricket teams. Then Stobswood used a field near to their present Welfare and later soccer was played at Widdrington Station until the 1960s but today the roles are reversed and once again Stobswood Welfare is home to the cricket and soccer teams. In 1989 the Welfare received a portion of a £1 million handout by the Opencast Executive for local villages and new changing rooms were built.

A fine 1950 photo of Widdrington Young People's Club. who played at the field near Whinney Crook and brought home the Coquetdale League Championship to the village. Back row: Aaron Morton, Jack Mavin, R. Jobson, Les Hawgood, Bill Morton, Arty Warwick, John Ryan, unknown. Front row: Bill Mather, Wilf Kelly, Jim Bolton, Bill Kelly, George Grainger.

Always in the running for honours this Stobswood cricket side of the early 1950s celebrating success at the Portland Hotel Ashington. Back row: Hugh Dane, J. Mclean, John Ireland, Hugh Weallans, Ron Willis, Jackson Storey, Ray Cook. Front row: Tony Fisher, Archy Morton, Billy Morton, Bill Rutherford, Ivor Dunn.

The 1950s were good years in the Coquetdale Leagues for the sport mad village teams and many awards added to their trophy cabinets and here is one of them. Back row: Jimmy Dunn (Senior), Jim Nichol, Jim Calder, Bob Waddell, Ray Kelly, Ray Todd, Billy Kelly, Jim Henderson. Front row: Bob Townsley, Jim Dunn (Junior), Rob Black, Jim Black, Ray Redpath.

## Cup Fever by Ray Brotherton

Stobswood Juniors had a cracking cup run during the 1955-6 season operating in the East North Junior League. We played our home matches in the field down past Whinney Crook at Widdrington and used an old railway carriage for a changing room. In the Northumberland Junior Cup we beat some of the best teams around including Seghill, Mickley, Newcastle St Mary's and in the final overcame North Shields Boys' Club 4-0 at Wallsend. The goals were scored by two Amble lads, 'Chicken' Brown scored a hat trick and Alder Hankin the other.

I remember after the game we paraded the County Cup down Wallsend High Street and later as our coach reached Stobswood someone opened the sliding roof and the trophy was on display through Widdrington, Red Row, Broomhill and Amble. After that everyone had the time of their life celebrating our success.

Sometime later a dinner was held to celebrate the winning of both the County and the League Cup at Widdrington Social Club when we were presented with our medals by Newcastle Directors Stan Seymour and Roddy McKenzie.

The victorious Stobswood Junior Team of 1955-6 who won the East Northumberland Junior League Cup and the Northumberland County Junior Cup with committee and supporters of the team. The team starting fourth left in the middle row are: Brian Riddell, Ray Brotherton, Ken Walton, John Thompson, Tommy Liddell, Alder Hankin. Front row: Shorty Allen, Billy Gray, Bill Hallowell, Edwin Kelly, Chicken Brown and Dennis Black sitting next to committee man Jim Bolton. The man on the right is Newcastle United Director Stan Seymour. Among other local faces are: Ken and Cec Middlemiss, Law Kelly, Jack Hall, Rutherford, Bob Redpath, Billy Bolton, Sep Simpson, Arty Warwick and Tommy Walton.

On to the early 1970s with a photo of Stobswood Welfare with what is thought to be the Northumberland Aged Miners' Homes Cup displayed at the Welfare Ground with Stobswood School in the background. In the back row: Derek Knox, Keith Tweddle, Alan Hay, Eddie Allen, Tony Jones, Andy Allen, Jim Stewart. Front row: Henry Douglas, Alan Morton, Derek Wanless, Ron Gibhard, Ian Allison.

# Grangewood First School

Opened on the 3rd September 1974 and available to 178 pupils on the 5th September the purpose built School catered for the area pupils to 11 years of age who moved from the old Stobswood Complex. The 65 remaining children who were taught in the Stobswood annexe came on the 14th May 1975. Headmaster was Mr Tait and Mrs Noble second in command who came from the Stobswood School.

A Victorian Day was held at the school with everyone dressed in period costume for the occasion and the whole School turned out for the photograph looking south to Grange Road.

Pat Lodge served as assistant cook at both Stobswood and Grangewood Schools for 22 years and was thanked for her efforts in 1988 when she retired. Pictured here in the centre with husband Stan and daughter Margaret holding gifts from School Staff and friends.

All female members of staff in this 1996 photo call. Included back row: Angela Brotherton, Susan Armstrong, Julie Herron, Carolyn Hepworth, Jennifer Clark, Eileen Jennings, Catherine Patterson. Front row: June Etterley, Susan Howe, Marion Rackham (Head), Sylvia Taynton, Joanne Davies.

Alistair McLean of RJB Mining presents a cheque to Grange View teachers Susan Howe, Julie Herron and Eileen Jennings in 1999, a much needed boost to the School's assets. RJB had previously found funding for extensions to the School's classrooms.

## Burnings and Burials

The Foot and Mouth epidemic that hit the County in February 1991 shook the Farming Community to the core, but to the folk of the local communities it was to be much more than that. The transport of bloody carcases to the designated Widdrington Burial Site and the burning of animal carcases on huge pyres at Druridge with the danger of toxic fumes and ash brought massive protests from the local villages. Fears over health and safety saw the formation of the Widdrington Liaison Group who campaigned and fought to have the procedures ended, a fight that lasted well into the following year.

Pickets were organised and petitions signed while leading Government and European Parliament Officials were lobbied on the situation.

A warm day in the summer of 2001 and pickets wait at the gates of the Widdrington Burial Site to vet the wagon loads of animal carcases that passed through. Young and old alike picketed with some prepared for a lengthy stay.

Right to the heart of things went these Widdrington protesters suitably dressed to make their point. Straight to the top man himself, Nick Brown in charge of the Governments slaughter and disposal operations at that time.

## Old Ferneybeds by the Mile

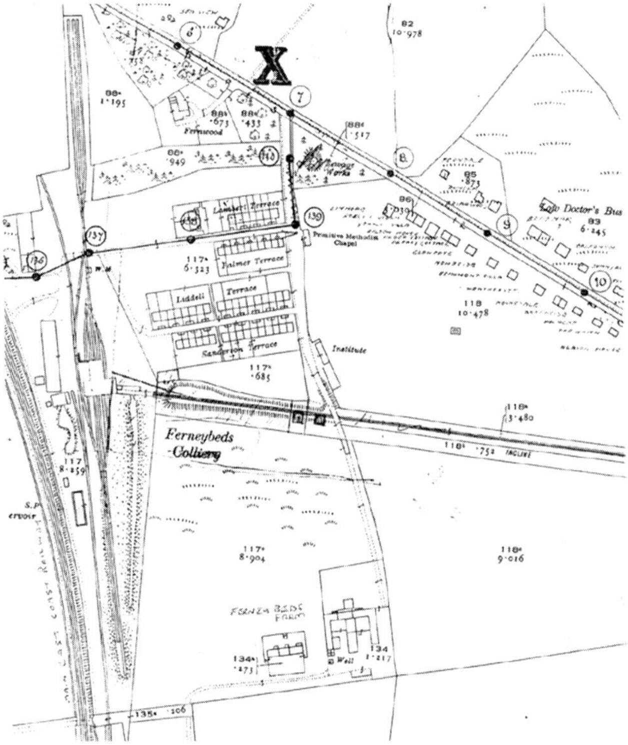


*Right*: The village in 1923 showing its position to the Colliery and the mile road at the top with some houses already built or in the process of construction.

The mile road in the 19th century and the early part of the 20th was used by the Cresswell family to travel by horse and trap from Cresswell Hall to Widdrington Station and the Baker Cresswells were recorded as being benefactors in maintaining the condition of the area roads.

The little enclave known as Ferneybeds owes its name to the bracken beds that existed in the area in ancient times. When the pit opened in 1909 there was much evidence of this in the fossils found in the strata. The model pit village evolved shortly after the pit commenced operations. Built and owned by the Widdrington Coal Company the four streets of houses, Lambert, Liddell, Sanderson and Palmer were named after the Coal Company's directors.

Described by the area Medical Officer of Health in 1911 as a model village that would set new standards in Public Health in Colliery villages, the village comprised of a Colliery Manager's house, two Under Managers' houses and 51 cottages.

A Methodist Chapel was erected which was a tin building that had been in use at the Colliery and carted to the village. The building was declared a designated place of worship in a service on the 15th January 1914. Mr Proudlock was a lay preacher there for many years. The Chapel partly amalgamated with Widdrington in 1967 and the building was pulled down in 1977. An Institute was provided for the Colliers opposite Sanderson Terrace.

*Left*: Three of the Hogg family who worked at the pit in this fine picture of circa 1920. Bob, John and Dick in typical pit attire with short hoggers, waistcoats and black store socks preparing for another shift underground.

*Left*: Sunday really was a day of rest for the colliery folk and kept that way with a chance to wear something a little different for Arthur, Dick and Bob Hogg at their Ferneybeds home and a watch and chain added a touch of class to the outfit.

Gordon Willoughby: 'Our family came to Ferneybeds in 1924, when my dad bought land as a smallholding at the sale of the Widdrington Coal Company assets. We lived in the Gables House which was the Ferneybeds Colliery Offices. This is where the Gables estate is today. Billy Boutflower lived at the Farm and there was a stone quarry in the fields. There was only three wooden shacks along the mile road and a handful of houses that I remember. I had the job of selling milk to the pitmen's wives along the rows from a gallon can. I went to school at Stobswood and helped out on the holding and at 14 years old drove a wagon for Longstaff.'

The Gables, former Colliery Offices, in 1926. The bricked up doorway is the wages office where the miners would collect their pay packets.

# Ferneybeds Colliery

A rare old photo of the sinkers in 1909. The pit was producing coal just five weeks after the first sod was cut. Note the coal tub on shaft landing and the heap of coal behind the three operators.

The shaft was sunk 69 feet to the Yard Seam which was the only one worked in the pit's short 15 year history. The coal seam was three foot nine inches thick with two others worked, both three foot six inches thick, producing house and steam coal. New plant was brought in and the pit was producing six to seven hundred tons a day. An airshaft was sunk to a depth of 75 feet where the first bungalow on the mile road now stands.

The manager in 1914 was William English with Jackson Storey as his undermanager The workforce grew and by 1923 there were 278 men employed in the operation. The first record of a fatality was in 1915 when R. H. Weddell lost his life followed by T Spowart in 1917 and J Telfer, J Noble, and J Rutherford in 1919. Sadly in 1924 the Widdrington Coal Company went into liquidation when 225 men were employed at the colliery and all assets including the model village of Ferneybeds were sold off at public auction.

Norman Morley: 'I started work at the pit in July 1923 at 14 years old and my first job was leading the ponies down the drift to the workings. The drift was built with Pegswood bricks. Then I worked on the rope haulage stopping the tub sets at the bottom by ringing a bell. I was only there for six months before the pit closed and I moved on to Stobswood Colliery.'

*Above*: The Old Ferneybeds Drift which went underneath the Mile Road seen here with a set of chummins ready to be hauled down to the Yard Seam workings.

WIDDRINGTON,
near MORPETH,
NORTHUMBERLAND.

THE WIDDRINGTON COAL Co., Ltd.,
IN LIQUIDATION.

*Particulars*
OF THE
**Freehold Model Village**
erected about 10 years ago.

MODERN DETACHED VILLA
WITH VACANT POSSESSION,
standing in about 4 acres of ground,
AND
THE SUBSTANTIAL BUILDINGS,
including Engine House, Fitters' Shop, Stores, Offices, Dwelling House, Stables, etc.,
TOGETHER WITH OVER
38 ACRES OF FREEHOLD LAND,
suitable for Small Holdings,
WHICH

**Thos. B. Sanderson, Son & Townend,**
WILL OFFER FOR
SALE BY PUBLIC AUCTION,
IN THE
**PROPERTY MART,**
12, ELDON SQUARE, NEWCASTLE-UPON-TYNE,
*ON THURSDAY, JUNE 19th, 1924,*
AT 3·30 P.M. PRECISELY.

*For further particulars or orders to view apply:—*

| Solicitors: | Auctioneers and Chartered Surveyors: |
|---|---|
| Messrs. WILKINSON & MARSHALL, 1, Mosley Street, Newcastle-upon-Tyne. | THOS. B. SANDERSON, SON & TOWNEND, 3–5, Mosley Street, Newcastle-upon-Tyne. |

*Left*: The Widdrington Coal Company sale catalogue in 1924. The weekly rental of the Ferneybeds houses at that time ranged from five shillings and nine pence for a home in Palmer Terrace to six shillings and sixpence for a home in Sanderson Terrace.

# SECTION FOUR

# STOBSWOOD

MAJOR OAK     AGE 1.500 YEARS. GIRTH 35 FEET. BASE 64 FEET.

A Major Oak that existed in the Stobswood and Widdrington Park long before farming ever came to these areas.

Known in the 17th century as Stobas the name derived from the stubs of old trees that existed from the great forest that was present in ancient times. In the Parish of Ulgham until recent years, it holds strong ties with Widdrington Station due to having the first education and religious facilities in the two settlements.

Farming was the main occupation until the latter part of the 19th century and the sinking of Stobswood Colliery. In 1881 there were only three farms and the Colliery village. Recorded as tenant farmers in 1887 were Mr Todd at East Stobswood and Chris Whinham who farmed Middle and West Stobswood.

## Pit Work

Bell Pits were in operation around Norwoods as early as the 17th century. This was not mining on a grand scale but simply bell shaped pits dug out the ground to claim coal seams that outcropped near the surface. The shape of the working meant that no roof supports were needed and it was easily filled in and a new pit sunk nearby.

Stobswood Colliery was sunk in 1875, the royalty purchased from Mr Taylor of Chipchase and the Colliers' houses built as the pit progressed. Manager of the Colliery in 1882 was Mr J. Johnson then John Buglass in 1887 with Ben Forbitser his Mechanical Engineer and J.H. Burn the mine owner.

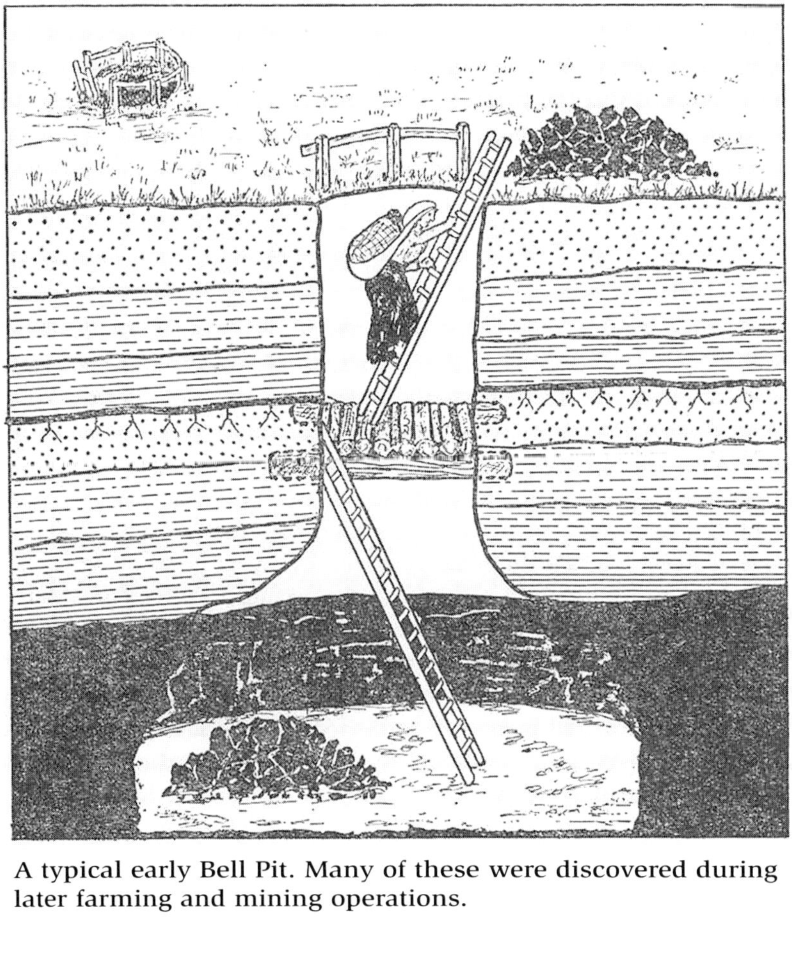

A typical early Bell Pit. Many of these were discovered during later farming and mining operations.

Stobswood Colliery in its early years showing the pit head and screening plant in close proximity to the main North Eastern railway network.

A disastrous fire in the latter part of the 1890s destroyed the headgear and buildings about the shaft area. There were two shafts at Stobswood both sunk to a depth of 300 feet, one for winding and the other for ventilation. Two drifts were sunk at Quarry and Northwood for ventilation and men travelling. In the early years coal produced was Steam but by 1940 Household coal was then mined. The Colliery had a small brickworks producing house bricks from the Seggar clay mined from the pit's Tilley and Yard seams. Most of the houses in the vicinity, pit buildings and social facilities were built with this distinctive straw coloured brick.

*Above*: Undaunted by the fire the owner soon ordered work to begin on the new shaft headgear and plant as seen in this postcard of around 1900. The lady in the foreground appears to be carrying her own coal home in two buckets.

Thomas Bewley became manager in 1914 and his undermanager was W.S. Rochester. It was 1930 when J.H. Spence took over with J. Storey as his understudy and the agent Mr Burn. Then in 1937 C. Hopper who was succeeded by Mr A. Defty in 1945 who is recorded as manager in 1950 with his assistant J.R. Jeffrey.

*Left*: An aerial bucket ropeway took waste from the pithead to be dumped on a heap and some of the young folk of the village actually took scary rides by clinging to the buckets and dropping off at convenient points.

Coal mining always has and will be a hazardous occupation. In the infant years of the local 19th century pits, sons followed fathers underground as young as 13 years of age with on the job training only minimal. Stobswood was no exception and injuries a common occurrence. Maiming and loss of life followed. It was in 1882 when the first death was recorded, that of James Sanderson and then in 1888 young Robert Lee a pony driver aged 14 was crushed by coal tubs. There were 21 deaths recorded at the colliery during its 90 year history but there may have been many more. Stobswood Colliery closed in 1965 at a time when over 300 men were employed there. This was the main reason for the eventual demise of the old Stobswood village.

Stobswood pithead was sited next to the main East Coast rail network and an unmanned railway crossing provided access. A recipe for disaster as these two snaps of the late 1940s show when a train smashed into a lorry on the crossing. The Colliery workshops are seen in the background.

The mangled remains of the lorry after it had been pulled clear of the wreckage on the pit side of the crossing.

*Above: Pathe News* came to Stobswood pit in the 1950s to film a team of old timers who were breaking production records. One of the set was Ogle Redpath who later received the MBE for his union services to the Coal Industry. Note the carbide lamp on his helmet. Carbide used to fuel the lamp could be bought from the Co-op out of the miner's wages.

*Left*: Every coal mine has its tragedies at some stage during operations and Stobswood was no exception with fires and accidents recorded during its history. Mines rescue teams were a necessary part of the set up and volunteers recruited and trained to the highest standards. Bob Tweddell and his marra are seen here preparing for a training exercise.

*Above*: Pictured at the pit in 1952 are these local craftsmen outside the workshops. Maintenance played a large part in the pit's operation and Blacksmiths Fitters and Electricians were employed underground and on the surface where much of the heavy repair work was carried out. Left to right: Keith Noble (Apprentice Blacksmith), T. Dunn (Striker), W. Richardson (Blacksmith), C. Watson (Fitter).

*Right*: Jimmy Richardson served as Foreshift Overman at Stobswood for many years. He is pictured here with daughter Flora outside his home in Grangewood Terrace around 1949.

Mrs Elliot: 'When young Gray was killed at the pit in 1924, Stobswood Band played a dirge and walked in front of his coffin which was resting on a cart pulled by horses with black plumes.'

George Mavin says: 'It was the 4th January 1940 when I started work on the screens at Stobswood then down the pit on the 5 am shift to couple tubs at the shaft bottom. From there it was inbye to the Yard Seam landings until at 16 I started as a spare putter and then onto cavil putting. I worked there for seven years until transferring to Ellington.'

John (Piper) Redpath: 'My first wage when starting work on the screens in 1939 was 10/9d a shift. I could earn more poaching rabbits for owld Mrs Trench who lived in the sinkers' houses near the pit. I remember one night when we used the nets and instead of rabbits a sheep got caught up and there was hell on that night.'

Flora Smith: 'I worked in the Wages Office from 1960 until just before the pit closed in 1965 when I was transferred to Linton Colliery. Mr Liddell was the pit manager and then Mr Hillier. Kath Sanderson worked there and Jack Oliver. Part of my job was putting up the miners' wages into little brass cups and giving them out on payday through the pay hatch window. All the money we received down to the last penny had to be accounted for and one day we were £5 short and all pays had to be checked but to no avail. The note was found later in the waste basket with the elastic band still attached, much to the relief of all the office staff.'

It wasn't all work and no play for the Stobswood workers as this 1960 snap shows as the employees enjoy a night out at the NCB dance at the Empress Ballroom, Whitley Bay. Left to right: Barbara and Harry Thompson who was the Baths Superintendent, Flora Richardson the wages clerk, George Harding Pit Timekeeper and two friends Mary and John Pringle.

## Night oot at Norwoods

The surface buildings at Stobswood's Norwoods drift housed the pit canteen and baths, but they were more than that to the mining families as they were allowed to be used on a Tuesday and Wednesday night as family nights. Meals could be bought at very reasonable prices during and after the second world war. There were said to be 274 steps down to the Stobswood workings.

## Tragedy at Norwoods

In 1995, thirty years after Stobswood Colliery closed, gas, in this case blackdamp claimed the life of Donald Tollett and his dog at the old Colliery buildings at Norwoods where once there had been an access drift to Stobswood Colliery workings. Donald had been at his brother's furniture factory housed in the old buildings and had gone to feed his horse which was stabled in a brick shed. Within a short time of entering the stable he and his dog were dead. It was thought that the dog was overcome by the gas which forms in layers near to the ground and had seeped through from the old mine. Mr Tollett probably bent down to tend to the animal and he too succumbed. The horse standing tall in his stall was unaffected.

*Right*: The bottom of the Old Park Drift was discovered when opencast coal operations started at Stobswood. Lots of local miners will have trod this way down the entrance to Stobswood Colliery.

## The Railway Murder

In 1910 Stobswood Coal Company offered a reward of £100 for evidence in the murder of John Innes Nisbet, Clerk Cashier to Stobswood Colliery. Nisbet had been travelling third class between Newcastle and Alnmouth on Friday 18th March with a black bag containing £370 9s 6d in gold, silver, and copper. He had been shot and his body stuffed under a seat when it was discovered later in the day by a porter at Alnmouth Station.

Police believed he had been killed between Stannington and Morpeth as fellow Colliery Cashiers had seen him alive when they left the train at Stannington. It was known that one passenger left the train at Morpeth who had a Stannington ticket and volunteered the twopence halfpenny excess fare.

Suspicion fell on John Dickman of Jesmond a former Colliery Wages Clerk who had been seen in the company of Nisbet at Newcastle Station but no one could definitely say he was the shadowy figure seen in John Nisbet's compartment. When arrested Dickman claimed he had travelled separately but admitted he had missed his stop at Stannington and set out on foot from Morpeth to return to Dovecote pit, Stannington to meet a contractor Mr William Hogg. However he had taken ill and not made the appointment returning to Morpeth to catch a train home. Dickman on his arrest had on his person £17 in gold coins and it was found that he was heavily in debt and had turned to gambling. More evidence showed that he purchased a hand gun by mail order. It appeared he had the means, motive and opportunity to commit crime. On June 9th the discovery of a black leather bag by Colliery Manager Peter Spooner at the bottom of an airshaft at Isabella Pit Hepscott with almost £1 of copper coins scattered around sealed Dickman's fate tying him to the scene of the crime.

Public feeling ran high during Dickman's three day trial and masses lined the streets of Newcastle as he protested his innocence. John Dickman was found guilty and after an appeal he was hanged at Newcastle Prison on August 10th 1910.

## Owld Stobswood Colliery Village

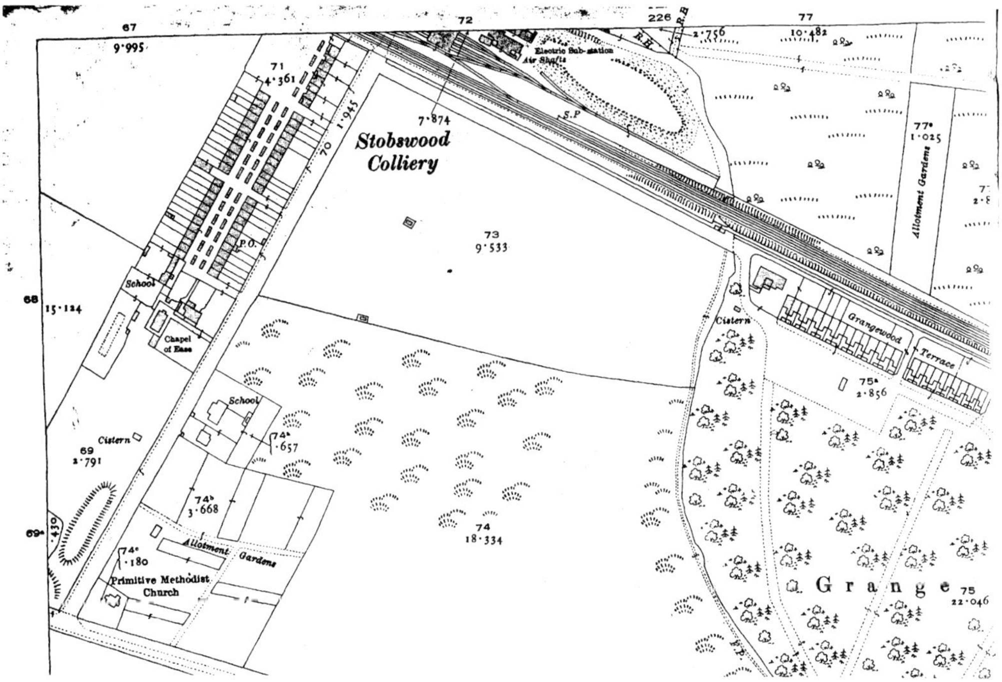


The 1923 map clearly shows the village top left in relation to the Colliery and the main East Coast Railway Line.

## Village Folk

An old postcard of Colliery folk around 1900 all neatly turned out ready for a trip to the coast, most probably to Druridge Bay by horse and cart, just as popular a venue now as it was then.

A wonderful old picture of Stobswood folk young and old in the 1920s and thought to be at a soup kitchen venue. This was the period in which there were two strikes affecting miners, one in 1921 and the other in 1926.

A cycling club existed in the village until well after the second world war and hail or shine it was off to coast or country every weekend for the locals. Here are four Stobswood lads taking a break after a run up the coastal route. Left to right: Bob Elliot, Jim Tweddell, Jackie Johnson, Robert Tweddell.

*Left*: In later years there was only two rows of houses, a front and a back Stobswood and a Wood Row behind the pit heap. Here we see two young blond residents Keith Noble and Norma Richardson in the summer of 1940 playing outside in the yard of a house in the front row.

*Below*: Two early Stobswood residents were John and Freddie Redpath who were members of the Morpeth Pipe Band and in great demand for functions of any kind. Here they are in their colours piping in the Northumberland Coal Queen at a Coal Board Luncheon at the Queens Head, Morpeth in the 1970s, supported by Union Officials Dennis Murphy, Sam Scott, and Labour MP Neil Kinnock

## Naughty Boy

On the 20th September 1918 George Little was fined 5 shillings for failing to display his name on his cart. Did the polis not naa there was a war on!

## Church, Chapel and School

A wooden hut was erected in 1882 and this was the first Church of England School in the Colliery and catered for 56 boys and girls, John Barker was head. There was a Sunday School and a Friday Band of Hope.

In 1895 the new Mission Church of the Good Shepherd was built with a foundation stone laid on March 30th and the Church dedicated on June 3rd. In 1906 the head of the School was then John C. Hodgson with the School Governors being the Rev Abner Rothwell Gregory, George Taylor and John Buglass. It was 1907 when land for use as a Public Elementary School was provided by landowner Thomas Taylor which was later named Stobswood Council School.

This is the neat little Mission Church School at Stobswood in the early 1900s. Note the bellcote at the front.

Stobswood bairns and teachers from group 4 in 1909 at the Council School with pupils of various ages.

Taken around 1919 outside the School, class 5 pose with the headmaster and two lady teachers. There may still be some of these children in the area today.

A 1920s snap of Stobswood pupils outside the big house next to the School in typical period dress with their lady tutor on the left.

All the 1923 School Football Team received was a shirt. It was up to them to supply shorts and socks to play in. The 11 lads and the head have somehow managed to sign on a young sub in case of injury.

## Old Stobswood Chapel

Stobswood Methodist Church, better known as the Chapel, was built in 1913 on land leased by Thomas Taylor. The lease to the trustees was for 99 years at a premium of £1 per year.

*Right*: Stobswood Methodist Church known to locals as the 'Tin Tabernacle' celebrating its 25th anniversary in 1938. Note the request for a silver coin at the foot.

After the Church closed in 1958 the organ was removed to the new Methodist Church at Widdrington Station. Found inside when cleaning the instrument in 1967 was an envelope containing a shilling from the old Church dated 1918.

Stobswood :: Methodist :: Church

25th ANNIVERSARY

1913 - 1938.

Saturday, April 23rd

JUMBLE SALE

In BENEVOLENT HALL at 2-30.

Admission 2d.

Sunday, April 24th,

SPECIAL SERVICES

2-30 p.m. 5-30 p.m.

Rev. L. METCALFE, Alnwick.

Monday, April 25th, at 2-30 p.m.

WOMEN'S MEETING

7 p.m. CONCERT IN CHURCH

STRIPPING OF SILVER TREE

BY MRS. BAIRD.

Please help us by adding a Silver Coin and a proverb to your envelope to be called for on April 22nd.

Portland Printing Co., Hindmarch (Printers) Ltd., Ashington.

## Woodburn, Grangewood

This area of Stobswood grew as the brickyard prospered and many of the officials were housed here and the Stobswood Miners' Institute and Old Age Miners' Cottages built in this area.

The Institute was opened by William Straker on 25th August 1933 to serve the social needs of a thriving Stobswood community. Records show that it was used as an overflow classroom for the Stobswood School during the 1940s.

A cosy woodland setting for the purpose built 'Tute' as locals named it. Not only did it house the usual social activities but had a shop that sold bread and sweets, a handy outlet for the local housewives.

The south facing games room with French windows giving a light and airy feel about the place. There were also rooms for billiards, table tennis and a reading room.

The Tweddell family lived in Grangewood and like most of the residents in the area either worked at the pit or the brickyard. Young Jim Tweddell is shown here in typical early 20th century pit lad's attire. Note the short hoggers above navy blue store stockings, a soft cap and the old oil-filled midgie lamp. One of the most crude forms of light, the dirty and smelly midgie had one benefit, it had a hook attached which was used to hang it from a pit prop while the collier worked.

*Below*: The Tweddell family of Grangewood in Sunday best outside their house with Jim front left and his brothers about 1920.

*Above*: Lots of Stobswood families here in this wedding party reception photo taken in the garden of Brickyard Manager Mr Heaslett's house in Woodburn. The bride and groom Flora Trench and Frank Queen, who was a Clerk for the Coal Board, are seen in the centre of the picture.

*Right*: A 1930s photo and coal was then delivered by horse and cart and tipped in the street by the coalhouse trapdoor ready to be shovelled inside. Here we see young Frank Queen giving the delivery man a helping hand at Woodburn.

*Above*: Old Grangewood residents John and Jane Lisa Queen who were celebrating their diamond wedding with all five of their sons, Bert, Stephen, Stan, Frank and Lance outside their home. Bert was the projectionist at the Co-op Hall Cinema and Lance was a well known music teacher.

*Left*: Four young Richardson girls in 1949 at their house in Grangewood, all very smart and dressed much the same in summer frocks. Left to right: Elaine, Norma, Margaret and Flora.

*Right*: Lots of Social History in this picture of a young girl in 1947 in Grangewood as she makes friends with the milk delivery horse standing in front of the old coalhouse trap door.

*Below*: Improvements to the Woodburn Childrens Play Park opposite the row of houses in 1999 was assisted by local mining firm RJB, just one of the many projects in the area in that year who received backing from this source.

# New Stobswood County Primary School

The new Stobswood school with its distinctive pantile roof was built around 1924 next to the cricket ground and was similar in many ways to the design of Linton and Lynemouth schools built by Carse and Sons some two years later. There were also huts around the main School and playground which served as extra classrooms, Library, Hall, Canteen and Gym. It catered for children of all ages until 1966 when the pupils over 11 years went to school at Hadston. When the Grangewood First School was built in 1974 this was the beginning of the end for Stobswood School which did still cater for a small number of children for a while and was then used as a storeroom until it was demolished.

Mrs Noble remembers: 'I had only been at the new school for a year before I left in 1925 at 14 years of age and the school had just opened when I went there.'

A large group of local youngsters in this Stobby School snap of 1929 with some of them still around today and many of their families resident in the area. Included are, back row: Rogers, Rogers, Davison, M. Hamilton, Robson, E. Willoughby, D. Aitken, French, Henderson, Morton, J. Foster, J. Harkins, G. Ferguson, Mr Atkinson (Head). Middle row: E. Henderson, Spowart, D. Davison, A. Hamilton, R. Black, Davison, Lindsay, Elliott, Lindsay, F. Foster, B. Nicholson, Davison, Douglas. Front row: Davison, J. Engels, A. Douglas, E. Robson, Robson, J. Black, G. Willoughby, J. French, Henderson, Henderson, J. Henderson, Rogers, Engels.

The girls' netball team and teacher of 1934 winners of the Amble Area Schools Shield with Nancy Black standing second left in the back row.

Miss Dickinson's class of upper infants in 1948 with two of the three rows of pupils named. Middle row: George Richardson, Vince Shepherd, Billy Henderson, Angela Spowart, Doris McInness, Mavis Holmes, Ann Redpath, Joan Hyslop, Billy Hindmarsh, John Middlemas, Ralph Aspey. Seated: Flora Richardson, Annie Mavin, Anne Barras, Brenda Telfer, Nola Patten, Anne Gowland, Irene Trench, Betty Fisher, Brenda Anderson, Peggy Henderson. Maureen Dodd, Olive Dean.

Around 1951 and many names to put to the faces of these Stobby and Widd pupils who would be about nine years of age then. Back row: Eddie Briggs, Jimmy Lytham, Jacky Mather, Shepherd, Wilfred King, unknown, Peter Dyne, Billy Lindsey, Lance Richardson, Arthur Grieves. Middle row: Ossie Rochester, Peter Cochrane, Gerry Patton, Olga Edmonds, Norma Richardson, Gwen Davison, Norma Calder, Elaine Wharton, Noreen Brodie, Ian Gordon, Robert Black, George Davis. Front row: Edith Queen, Vivien Rogers, Doris Trench, Anne King, Estelle Rutherford, Pat Forster, Valerie ?, Joan Elliott, Monica Warwick, Susan Boxall, Noreen Hindmarsh, Shirley Easton.

Most girls played netball and Stobswood had its fair amount of success over the years as did this young team of 1952 who were not too fussy about footwear as long as they were on the team. Back row: Flora Richardson, Julie ? Vera Brown, ?. Front row: Angela Spowart, Betty Fisher, Irene Trench, Joan Hyslop.

A cracking 1957 shot of long serving teacher Mrs Tait's class and many local children here still around the area.

Mr Ramsey and his class around 1957 and for the lads it's all about change at this time from short pants to long trousers and smart pullovers.

Lots of the village ladies in this photo call of the 1960s which includes Canteen Staff and helpers who assisted with the young folks meals. Back row: I. Purdom, Lily Neave, Marie Craig, Jean Briggs, Pat Lodge, M. Barker. Front row: Margaret Bruce, Marion Bertram, Mr Clark (Headmaster), Mrs Noble, Pat Anderson.

Much respected Headmaster Mr Harry Clark on his retirement in July 1967 is congratulated by Elaine Richardson in the Schoolyard with pupils and staff looking on. Harry got his wish and was presented with an armchair by the teachers and pupils.

The smartly dressed teaching staff at Stobswood School some thirty years ago and some of them still living in the vicinity today. Back row: June Lawson, Ada Ridley, Ann Croft, Nora Matheson, Evylyn Dixon. Front row: Jack Ramsey, Christine Carvill, Joan Tait, George Tait (Head), Jean Gagie, Margaret Leidiard, Margaret Noble.

Joan Leithhead who now lives in Ulgham shown here with her class around 1972 and lots of the local children pictured wearing white socks, sandals and sandshoes. Rain, hail or shine all of the youngsters from Widdrington would take the route down the narrow path along by the main railway line to school.

Margaret Noble began teaching at Stobswood in 1966 and has many memories of her years at Stobswood serving with head teachers Mr Clark and Mr Tait. Margaret is seen here with her young pupils circa 1970 when she was appointed Deputy Head before transferring to the new Grangewood School in 1975.

Nora Matheson with her class of youngsters circa 1960s. Included in this snap are back row: Graham Ayre, Paul Cookson, John Defty, John Ashworth, Roger Cookson, George Embleton. Second back row: Ann Tait, Susan Mclean, Julie Hogg, Kim Middlemiss, Wendy Millican, Corinnia Townsley. Second front row: Julie Shepherd, Tracy Brooks, Wendy Batson, Heather Burton, Carol Shepherd, Jane Hedley, Helen Black, Sharon Dodds. Front row: Mark Henderson, Ray Bell, Christopher Blaydon.

## Stobswood & Widdrington Boys' Club by Rudi Lux

I came to Widdrington in 1956 and after a while started work at the Stobswood brickyard and later became a Foreman there. It was in 1959 that I took over the reins as Boys' Club Leader from Mr Morton. It was to be the start of what were happy and rewarding years of working with the young people of the area.

The activities were many and varied ranging from arts and crafts to the ultimate acclaim for the lads which were the Duke of Edinburgh awards. Peter Vaughan of Burn Fireclay Company was President and Treasurer with a strong committee formed from the local people. It may seem a little strange but we also had a girls' section which proved very successful. This came about in the 60s when St Mary's Church Hall closed and the girls who were in the Youth Club there were allowed by the education authorities to join the Boys' Club. I remember one amusing incident when the singer Frankie Vaughan who was president of the NABC came to a ceremony at the Club. He was a Jew and I an ex-German prisoner of war. The committee were not so sure how we would react to one another but their fears were foundless and all went well.

Football was always popular and I ran two teams, one in the East Northumberland Junior League and one operated in the Morpeth Sunday League with much success over the years. To raise funds for our club I ran a bingo at the hut and also took turns with Stobswood Welfare FC with a bingo night in the store hall. The members raised a lot of money with marathon runs and much of this was for charity. 1970 was a special year when the youngsters raised funds and prepared a hardcourt and play area outside the headquarters which opened that year. Presentation nights at the Club were great nights when almost all the families of the area were represented. When I retired in 1975 I had spent 16 years as leader of Stobswood and Widdrington Boys' Club.

Awards were a regular occurrence for these boys' club members during the 60s and 70s, pictured at a ceremony at there headquarters. Left to right: D. Brown, E. Jones, D. Thompson, A. Plaice, area leader Mr Grey, and boys' club leader Rudi Lux.

All local lads in this soccer team who won the Morpeth Sunday League second division title in the 1972-3 season. Back row: A. Farrell, N. Gibbard, J. Bolton, J. Farrell, L. Edward, R. Gibbard, R. Lux. Front row: J. Morton, J. Boulding, K. Fraser, J. Dawson, G. Orgill, F. Douglas.

Little did the lads know that when they walked all the way from Edinburgh to Morpeth in relays to raise funds for Stannington Children's Hospital that a mouse who had found his way into the pram they pushed would stay with them the whole of the 124 miles journey which took 30 hours. This photo at the end of the journey shows the walkers and leaders at the Hospital. Back row: K. Hunter, R. Lux, D. Richardson, I. Richardson, C. Lux, S. Redpath, B. Parkinson, B. Simpson, D. Airey. Front row: P. Final, J. Douglas, I. Bruce.

At the launching of Boys' Club week in 1973, Stobswood lad Stephen Redpath was chosen to present a message from Lord Ridley to National Boys' Club representative and European Boxing Champion Joe Bugner at the Royal Festival Hall. A proud day for the lad and for the Boys' Club. Stephen is seen here on the left with Joe Bugner and lads from other regions who also presented messages.

*Above*: Funds for a hard court were raised by marathon runs by the boys themselves who also prepared the groundwork. Here are a group of local members at the opening in 1970 who just can't wait to try out a football on the new facility.

*Left*: 15 year old Irene Storey was the only girl member of a 12 strong team who completed a 130 mile marathon from Morecambe to Morpeth. Running in stages through the night the youngsters completed the journey in fourteen and a half hours. They raised £180 for their club and the mayor of Morpeth's Charity Appeal Fund.

# The Burn Fireclay Company

An aerial view of Stobswood brickyard centre right showing its position close to the pit with the main line running diagonally across the photo next to both with Grangewood and Woodburn to the west of the railway. Stobswood School and Welfare are seen centre left and the pit heap top left.

The new brickworks built to the east of the Colliery in 1923 proved to be a master plan for the Burn family who also owned the pit. Mr Boyle was the first manager at the plant which was then only producing building brick. In 1927 Mr James Heaslett was appointed as manager and firebrick was brought into production which along with other modern techniques made the brickworks and Stobswood Colliery highly profitable as they used the coal from their own pit and the excess coal and fireclay easily sold even in the depression years of the 20s and 30s which meant full time work for its employees.

The Burn family were noted as good employers and the Colliery and the brick works were virtually free from industrial action. The directors in 1938 were J.H. Burn, H.J.D. Burn and R.S. Burn.

Annie Mcinnes: 'I remember starting work at the brickyard shortly after it opened and among the many jobs I had were cleaning, carrying from new and dressing bricks. John Henry Burn was a nice man and a proper gentleman who would visit the plant each week and take time to speak to all his workers.'

**Bloody Hard Work by Jim Calder**

I worked on piecework at the brickmaking machine which made the wetbricks. There were three of us in a team plus a mixer man. My marras were Ray Todd and Frank Queen. Number One machine could turn out 10,500 bricks a shift. It was non-stop wheeling bricks to be fired in the kilns. It was hard work and you had to be fit just as we were. We were making canny money about £8 a week until I went into the army in 1953. My dad was a fireman at the yard and my brother Bill and sister Rita also worked at the brickyard. A bus load of Ashington lasses and one from Red Row would come every morning and they would clock in at 7.30 am. There were lots of Poles employed there and they were all good workers. Before they got houses they slept in the Canteen. The cook at the canteen was Mrs Walton.

When the country's pits were nationalised in 1947 this had a major impact on the brickworks as they now had lost their own source of raw materials from Stobswood Colliery. This saw the Burn family purchasing a mine and royalty at Causey Park and later at Ulgham.

When Stobswood Colliery was closed by the National Coal Board in 1965 the Burn Fireclay Co became the major employer of local people in the area until falling sales in the 1990s saw the company go into voluntary liquidation in December 1999 with the loss of almost 80 jobs.

A contented squad of men outside the kilns waiting to dispatch yet more bricks. Just look how near the Colliery was to the works with the pit shaft looming in the background.

Arnie Robson and his mate inside the works stacking bricks.

And yet more bricks inside the kiln waiting for dispatch while the team take a break, including George Turner, Jack Sim, Kit Pierce and Geordie Gair.

It was 1986 and a new kiln was being built. Surveying the scene are on the left one of the Director's sons and Widdrington man Rudi Lux who helped lay the founds and new rail track.

The brickworks as they are today, most of the buildings derelict. A new footbridge now spans the East Coast Railway Line. The plant is now earmarked for demolition in the near future.

# Section Five

# Opencast

## Coaling With The Sunshine Boys

A bird's eye view of the Sisters Opencast Coal Site between Stobswood and Widdrington Colliery showing the contours around the void. Top left is Stobswood Brickyard with the pit heap centre top and centre right Widdrington Colliery Disposal Depot.

The Widdrington area has been subject to the presence of open cast mining for over 60 years, long before the closure of Stobswood Colliery in 1965. The need for more coal to power the war effort saw the first opencast site at Ferneybeds in 1942 with most of the area being exploited at some period right up to the present site at Stobswood. Costain, Dowsett and Mcalpine were some of the early contractors around the village sites but gradually Crouch Mining took a leading role until the company folded in 2004.

The present day Stobswood site, the largest in the country, has employed almost 400 workers and extracted over 12.2 million tonnes of coal since it started operations in 1990. Now that coal extraction is coming to an end here further plans for an extension to the north are being considered which if granted will see work there completed by 2008 and the finish of Opencast Coal Mining in the Widdrington Area.

It was 1957 when contractor Derek Crouch released the giant excavator 'Big Geordie' at the Radar North site which gobbled up 75 tons of material in its massive bucket at one sweep. The fact that this monster could be fitted with two huge walking feet to move from site to site revolutionised the art of opencast mining in the area.

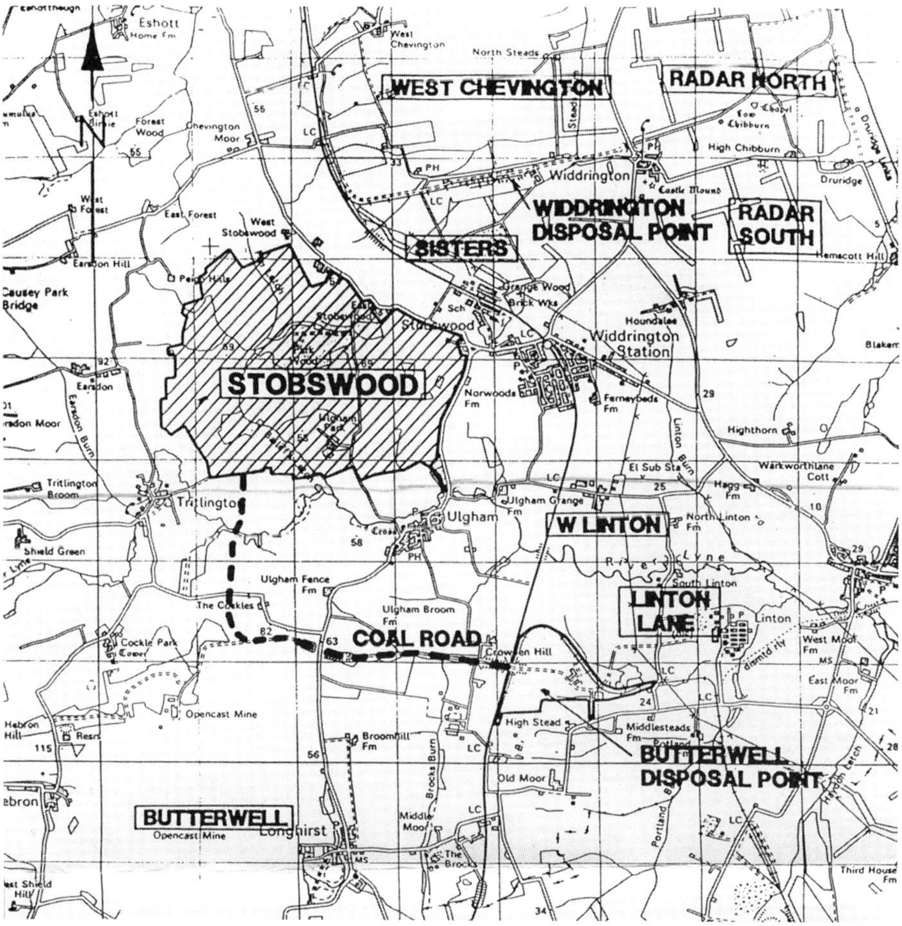


Many of the sites and disposal depots around the Widdrington area are featured on this map and show the scale of the Stobswood operation which covered 650 hectares.

Derek Crouch had their own transport to ferry coal from the disposal depots, shown in this grand photo of three men and a gem of a steam engine.

The Marian Dragline is shown minus its jib which it shed one day; I believe this was on a Friday the 13th during the 1950s while working the Radar South Site. Like any industry there is always the threat of accidents and on this occasion in a big way.

*Left*: A 1970s photo of Derek Crouch officials in the gigantic bucket of 'Big Geordie' at the Seven Sisters site.

*Below*: Officials and workers pose at the foot of 'Geordie'. Front row, includes: Alfie Bell (electrical), George Ashton (plant manager), Digger Lister (plant director), Bomber Brown (labourer), Jack Angus (cableman), Peter Falconer, Eddie Wilde (site manager), Chris Raine, Larry Ling (managing director). Back row: Ronnie Vickers (driver) Chris Montgomery, Paul Final, George Fisher, John Hickey, Monty Durham (dozer driver), Hughie Dane, Bill Curry, (chauffer), Colin Robson.

*Right*: Big Geordie was fitted with legs to walk from site to site and here he is on the epic journey from Widdrington to the new Butterwell operation. This was in September 1977 on a journey which took three weeks while the preparation took much longer with bridges built, hedges removed, the River Lyne dammed and many other operations which saw him arrive only a day late.

*Below*: An even bigger Dragline, the son of Geordie and named the 'Ace of Spades' by local schoolchildren was introduced to the Stobswood site and now stands visible for miles around waiting to hear what fate has in store for it. Too big for any other site in the country its future lies in work abroad. Seen here on site, it can take a 100 tons of material with one bite of its bucket.

The Stobswood site showing the exposed coal ready to be claimed. From the Beaumont to the Widdrington Yard Seam, Stobswood has worked 28 seams in all varying in thickness from six inches to four feet.

Nicknamed the 'sunshine boys' as opposed to the colliers in the deep mines it is not always that way weather wise for the opencast lads. Hail rain or shine, work goes on in most conditions. Taking time out for a photo call are this team at Stobswood. Shovel Driver is Gary Redfearn while back row are: Brian Dinning, Steven McGill, Stuart Freeman, John Leathley and site manager Peter Millar. Front row: Chris Collier, David Harrigan, Finlayson.

Site visits are the norm for anyone interested in the process and in this case it's the *Blue Peter* TV presentation team headed by Matt Baker who came to film in the bowels of the Stobswood workings, shown here being escorted around the site by Supervisor Charlie Cooper on the right.

Public relations always to the fore as seen here at this presentation when the then owners of the operation RJB Mining awarded a £200 cheque to Stobswood Junior Football Club members standing in front of a picture of the 'Ace of Spades'.

## Dig This

It was the 18th December 1987 when local people lost a campaign against British Coal to extract 11 million tons of coal at Stobswood Opencast site over 1,130 acres of land.

23rd May 1989. A million pounds given by the Opencast Executive for the villages of Stobswood, Widdrington Station and Ulgham. Alan Beith in talks to improve roads and a new Widdrington Community Centre.

Thursday 13th January 1992. Last shovelful of coal from Butterwell site.

2004. Production coming to an end at Stobswood site, application for further site until 2008 to the North submitted. Plans afoot to turn Stobswood void into a major Leisure Complex.

On the 7th September 2004 Northumberland County Council refused planning permission from UK Coal for an extension to their coaling operations. UK Coal are considering an appeal.

After opencast and the land returned to wildlife and farming in this shot taken from Druridge links looking to Chibburn Priory and on to the old village of Widdrington.